GOD'S PURPOSE FOR YOU

ANSWER LIFE'S FIVE KEY QUESTIONS

FUCHSIA PICKETT

Charisma
HOUSE
A STRANG COMPANY

GOD'S PURPOSE FOR YOU by Fuchsia Pickett
Published by Charisma House
A part of Strang Communications Company
600 Rinehart Road
Lake Mary, Florida 32746
www.charismahouse.com

Unless otherwise noted, all Scripture quotations are from the King James Version of the Bible.

Scripture quotations marked NIV are from the Holy Bible, New International Version. Copyright © 1973, 1978, 1984, International Bible Society. Used by permission.

Scripture quotations marked NKJV are from the New King James Version of the Bible. Copyright © 1979, 1980, 1982 by Thomas Nelson, Inc., publishers. Used by permission.

Cover design by Rachel Campbell
Interior typography by Sallie Traynor

Library of Congress Cataloging-in-Publication Data

Pickett, Fuchsia T.
 God's purpose for you / Fuchsia T. Pickett.
   p. cm.
 ISBN 0-88419-967-3
1. Providence and government of God--Meditations. 2.
Christian life--Meditations. I. Title.
 BT135.P48 2003
 248.4--dc21

                    2003007447

This book was previously published as *God's Dream* by Destiny Image Publishers, ISBN 1-56043-028-1, copyright © 1991.

03 04 05 06   87654321
Printed in the United States of America

It takes a "special man" of strength, security and stamina to be the husband of a woman minister, teacher and writer. Leroy is that man. Though he physically is unable to do so now, he has functioned invaluably in our ministry, especially in the production of manuals, tapes and books. The message he preaches in the living of his life is one of total commitment to the mandate God has laid upon our lives.

I am grateful to God for his love, encouragement and total support.

Contents

Foreword by Judson Cornwall. vii

Introduction. 1

1 Purpose at Great Cost 4

2 God's Purpose Confirmed. 22

3 Cultivating God's Purpose. 34

4 Called to God's Purpose 47

5 The Character of God's Purpose 58

6 Purpose Unencumbered by Tradition. . . . 74

7 Purpose Redeemed 86

8 God's Purpose Fulfilled 104

Foreword

In the mid-seventies, I invited a woman evangelist to my church for the weekend. Fuchsia Pickett's ministry was so electrifying that we extended her stay for three weeks. She used our church for many months as her headquarters while God directed her ministry through various churches on the West Coast. It was the beginning of a friendship that has become a brother/sister relationship in the Lord.

Our roles were reversed many years later when I made my headquarters in her church in Plano, Texas. For several of those years, I served as an assistant pastor to the congregation. Now God has again released Fuchsia Pickett to the larger body of Christ as a mother in Israel. Her academic background and years of experience as a teacher, evangelist and pastor have given her insights desperately needed in the church today.

This book is the heart of the message that God has burned into the soul of this precious woman. She has envisioned the reality of God's eternal purpose. When people embrace this truth, it becomes life changing. I have heard her share these principles in many different situations, and it has always produced life and inspired action.

If this book can accomplish the same results that miraculously occur when she presents these truths in person, it will become a channel for revitalizing pastors, elders, deacons and lay workers. In turn, the entire church will be revived. Read this book with a prayerful attitude and allow God to effect changes in you. Study the principles shared and search them out in your Bible.

I highly commend the author to you as a woman of the Word, a person of integrity and one who lives what she preaches.

JUDSON CORNWALL, TH.D.
PHOENIX, ARIZONA

INTRODUCTION

When God begins to pour out of His Spirit, God's children will come into a full understanding of His purpose for the earth—and for each believer. You can grasp God's purpose for you and set your heart to fulfill it as you begin to see the eternal plan that was predestined by the Council of God before the foundation of the world. You can be filled with a deep longing to see God's purpose for you—and for the earth—fulfilled. That intense desire will become a motivating force for action.

Fulfilling God's purpose for him was the driving force of the apostle Paul's life. Catch a glimpse of his deep desire to please God from his words in Ephesians 3:

> For this cause I Paul, the prisoner of Jesus Christ for you Gentiles…was made a minister, according to the gift of the grace of God given unto me by the effectual working of his power…that I should preach among the Gentiles the unsearchable riches of Christ…To the intent that now unto the principalities and powers in heavenly places might be known by the church the manifold wisdom of God, *according to the eternal purpose which he purposed in Christ Jesus our Lord.*
> —EPHESIANS 3:1, 7–8, 10–11, EMPHASIS ADDED

Paul believed that every believer should be filled with

this intense desire to fulfill the purposes of God for his or her life. He spoke of it to his spiritual son, Timothy, by saying, "[He] hath saved us, and called us with an holy calling, not according to our works, but according to his own purpose and grace, which was given us in Christ Jesus before the world began" (2 Tim. 1:9). Then he admonished Timothy: "That good thing which was committed unto thee keep by the Holy Ghost which dwelleth in us" (v. 14).

What was God's purpose…His dream? The great heart of God had a dream that was born out of His need. Although some theology teaches that God has no need because of the fact of His self-existence, I believe, by definition, we can establish that God had a need. God is love. Love needs someone who can become a recipient, one who can respond to that love. In order to meet that need, God had a *dream* for a family that would be made in His image, and into whom He could pour Himself.

Having determined to have a family, the triune Godhead made a sworn covenant among Themselves that that dream would be fulfilled, judicially setting full redemption to our account before mankind was ever created or time established.

But before this fundamental purpose could be fulfilled, God's own beloved Son must make the ultimate sacrifice. He must die that we could live. He must break the death grip of Satan to give us eternal life. In 1 John 3:8 we read:

> For this purpose the Son of God was manifested,
> that he might destroy the works of the devil.

How incalculable must have been the suffering endured when Jesus became the Lamb, slain in the heart of God from the foundation of the world. (See Revelation 13:8.) The Godhead had to suffer that *hurt-love* in order for God's purpose for mankind to be fulfilled. That sacrificial love initiated the completion of God's eternal purpose to bring many sons into glory.

The Scriptures give glimpses of this wonderful plan from earliest history. However, that covenant purpose was not completely unveiled until God revealed the mystery of the church to the apostle Paul, who declared, "...the mystery, which from the beginning of the world hath been hid in God" (Eph. 3:9). God unveiled His eternal purpose, revealing what He has done, is now doing and will do. His desire for a family is destined to be fulfilled. God will have a family in His own image, revealed through Jesus, the express image of His person. It is my prayer that you will determine to become a part of fulfilling God's purpose for mankind by understanding and completing God's purpose for you! For this cause you were created.

Chapter 1

PURPOSE AT
GREAT COST

M y entire life was changed by the discovery of this one truth: The destiny of my life is hinged upon understanding God's eternal purpose, which He unveiled to man through His hurt-love.

I was not aware of this powerful truth, despite the fact that I had finished my graduate studies in theology, including rewriting the five hundred cardinal doctrines of the church for my thesis. Through my studies, I had learned how to investigate the great truths of the Bible and thought I knew something about almost every doctrine. I prided myself on my attempts to be an exegetical theologian, pastoring and carefully teaching the Word in Bible colleges for seventeen years.

However, it wasn't until after I received the baptism of the Holy Spirit, which brought me into a greater relationship with the divine Teacher, that I discovered the great truth of the critical importance of understanding God's eternal purpose.

Truth has the incredible power to free man of despair, hopelessness and a meaningless existence, and to create in him a sense of destiny and purpose that can motivate him to greatness. Jesus said of Himself,

"I am...the truth" (John 14:6). To believe in Jesus involves receiving the truth of His teachings and allowing them to change your thinking, your values and your behavior. The works of the devil—the lies that are working in your life to destroy you—are only exposed as they are contrasted with truth. In the light of truth, those lies lose their seductive power, and you are set free from their destruction.

Freedom is the scriptural promise to all who walk in truth. "Ye shall know the truth, and the truth shall make you free" (John 8:32). That promise gives each of us hope to become the person God intended us to be as we walk in His truth. If you want to know real meaning and purpose in your life, your home and your church, it is necessary that you pursue God's truth.

THE FIVEFOLD CRY OF THE HUMAN HEART

There is a dynamic truth in the Bible that has been pivotal to my life. It is that within the heart of every person ever born is a fivefold cry answered only by an understanding of God's eternal purpose for mankind. This heart cry asks the following questions:

- "Who made me?"
- "Who is God?"
- "What is the purpose of my life?"
- "How can I fulfill my destiny?"
- "After this life, what is there?"

These questions are so simple that we stumble over them, yet so profound that if we cannot answer them we simply exist, without any true sense of direction or meaning for our lives. Until we properly answer these questions we do not know we are people of destiny, born at the exact time God intended that we be born. When we discover answers to these questions, our search for identity is over. We know who God is and who He meant us to be.

As soon as children are old enough to ask questions, they begin to wonder where they came from and who made them. Many do not receive satisfactory answers to these questions in the schools or churches they attend. As teenagers they may turn to drugs, promiscuous sex, even suicide, searching desperately for their identity. (I do not believe anyone would ever commit suicide if they understood the truth of God's eternal purpose.) Later, as college students, their professors offer them various philosophies in an attempt to answer these basic questions, without success. Still searching for truth, many turn to Eastern religions, hoping to find answers that will satisfy their hearts' cry. Failing to find the answers they seek, which cannot be found apart from knowing God, many people live in a frustration that ends in hopelessness and despair.

A man in my congregation in Texas acknowledged that the extraordinary success he was enjoying in his life and career was because of his understanding of God's eternal purpose. He had attained everything a man could want before he reached the age of forty. In his address to a distinguished audience on the occasion of accepting the presidency of a large corporation, he declared, "I received my training and degrees from a university, but I did not prepare for this position through my university training. The teaching of my pastor, who showed me God's eternal purpose, put my life on pivot. I am prepared to take this position because I know who made me, who I am, why I am here, and how this position relates to those issues." His life was given purpose by his understanding of God's eternal plan for him.

What does that plan involve, and how does the understanding of it influence the destiny of a life? To answer that question, let's allow our imaginations to take us back into the eons of eternity, to the "beginning," to listen to the triune Godhead as They expressed a deep desire among Themselves. Because of who God is, He had a need. Though our theological understanding of God's self-existence, which pictures God as having need of nothing, often prevails in our thinking, all Scripture testifies to the contrary, showing us that God had a need.

"God is love" (1 John 4:8). Love is not merely an attribute of God's character, but the essence of His being. The nature of love requires a recipient, one who will respond by choice to the love given. Because God is love, He needed someone to respond to His love. Because of that longing, They said among Themselves, "Let us make man in our image" (Gen. 1:26). God expressed His need in His desire for a family, one into whom He could pour His very nature. His purpose in creating mankind was to have someone with whom to fellowship and share His love. He desired a family who would have His "family spirit" and would choose to respond to His love. He did not create a robot to love Him automatically, for, by definition, love does not force someone to respond with love. God wanted a family who would choose to love Him.

In eternity, the three members of the Godhead took an intertheistic covenant and swore among Themselves that God's purpose would be fulfilled. They became totally involved in bringing that covenant to pass—to fulfill God's dream for a family. God later revealed this covenant to Abraham, as the Book of Hebrews tells us: "When God made promise to Abraham, because he could swear by no greater, he sware by himself" (Heb. 6:13). God needed no man to swear by; They swore by each other. Having confirmed the covenant with an oath in eternity, the triune Godhead had initiated among Themselves their dream for a family.

There was equality among the three members of the Godhead in eternity, as we understand when we read of Christ Jesus, "Who...thought it not robbery to be equal with God" (Phil. 2:6). We read of that equality in the first verse of John: "In the beginning was the Word, and the Word was with God, and the Word was God" (John 1:1). However, God's plan for a family would affect that equality as the Father looked beyond Adam's disobedience to make provision for the redemption of mankind, whom They were going to create in Their image. God's eternal purpose was decreed, willed, purposed and predestined before man was created. In the corridors of eternity, Jesus came out of the Godhead as the Son of God, suffering His *kenosis* to become the "Lamb slain from the foundation of the world" (Rev. 13:8). That emptying of Himself, of which we read in the second chapter of the Book of Philippians, happened first in eternity.

It cost the Godhead inestimable suffering to bring Their love to us. One of our favorite Bible verses reveals the pain involved in bringing God's love to man. As children we learn to quote, "For God so *loved* the world, that he gave his only begotten Son, that whosoever believeth in him should not perish, but have everlasting life" (John 3:16, emphasis added). This is a statement of hurt-love. We cannot comprehend the suffering of God in eternity. God knew that man would fail the love test, and that Jesus would have to become the sacrificial Lamb to redeem us unto Himself—causing God to suffer incalculable loss. Yet so great was God's need for someone into whom He could pour His love that He proceeded to fulfill His dream to have a family.

THE LAMB OF GOD

God's hurt-love produced the nature of the Lamb. His family would share His nature, the Lamb Spirit of hurt-love. Jesus came, not to save us from hell, but to give the Father a family that would reflect the nature of the Father's love. To accomplish that purpose, Jesus became the Lamb of God, slain in the heart of God.

In the types of the Old Testament, we see the suffering heavenly Father each time a man had to choose his own spotless lamb, tie it with a cord and take it to the temple to offer it as a sacrifice. He is walking with that prepared paschal lamb, tied with a cord. He comes with a hurt-love, bringing His Lamb to slaughter in order to redeem us. God's heart is beating with a longing to impart to us the same quality of love that the Godhead enjoyed in eternity. Is it any wonder the highest order of worship found in the Book of Revelation is expressed in the cry, "Worthy is the Lamb that was slain to receive power, and riches, and wisdom, and strength, and honour, and glory, and blessing" (Rev. 5:12)?

God gave us a beautiful eightfold picture of His Lamb in the Scriptures to portray vividly His plan of redemption of mankind.

1. Peter showed us the lamb of *predestination.* The apostle Peter wrote: "Redeemed…with the precious blood of Christ, as of a lamb without blemish and without spot: who verily was foreordained before the foundation of the world" (1 Pet. 1:18–20).

2. We see the lamb of *paradise* in the Garden of Eden, where blood was shed to clothe Adam and Eve with animal skins. From then on, all sacrificial offerings looked back to the one made by Jehovah-Jesus in the Garden of Eden, and forward to the sacrifice Christ was to make on Calvary.

3. Abraham and his son Isaac discovered the lamb of *promise* after they ascended the slopes of Mount Moriah to worship. Isaac asked his father, "Where is the lamb for a burnt offering?" (Gen. 22:7). Abraham answered, "God will provide himself a lamb for a burnt offering" (v. 8).

4. The *Passover* lamb was revealed to the children of Israel on the night when the death angel visited the firstborn of Egypt. (See Exodus 12.)

5. When John the Baptist saw Jesus coming to the Jordan and declared, "Behold the Lamb of God, which taketh away the sin of the world" (John 1:29), he alluded to the lamb the Hebrews offered as a sacrifice every morning and evening in their ritual of worship—the lamb of *pardon*.

6. The lamb of *propitiation* was revealed in the Hebrews' celebration of the Day of Atonement.

7. The lamb of *prophecy* was seen by Isaiah when, under the prophetic inspiration of the Holy Spirit, he declared, "He is brought as a lamb to the slaughter" (Isa. 53:7).

8. Finally, on the historical cross of Calvary, we saw the lamb *provided*.

In the Lord Jesus, God fulfilled every promise, every prophecy, every sacrificial type found in the Bible. That day at Calvary, the Father was still leading His lamb, all the way to the cross, to fulfill His purpose and bring His dream to pass.

The most wonderful love story ever told is the story of God's love. All mankind is part of God's purpose to have a family: "According as he hath chosen us in him before the foundation of the world…having predestinated us unto the adoption of children by Jesus Christ to himself, according to the good pleasure of his will" (Eph. 1:4–5). Every person who would ever be born was in God's mind in eternity when He initiated that purpose. Your name was not written in the Lamb's Book of

Life when you received Jesus as your Savior. It was written there before the foundation of the world.

From eternity, God willed that no person on earth should perish. He recorded every name. God said to Jeremiah the prophet, "Before I formed you in the womb, I knew you" (Jer. 1:5, NIV). The psalmist David declared, "My frame was not hidden from you when I was made in the secret place. When I was woven together in the depths of the earth, your eyes saw my unformed body. All the days ordained for me were written in your book before one of them came to be" (Ps. 139:15–16, NIV). God knew us before we were born, and He ordained that we would have life.

Your name will only be blotted out of the Lamb's Book of Life if you do not choose to have the life of God. In the Book of Revelation we read, "He that overcometh, the same shall be clothed in white raiment; and I will not blot out his name out of the book of life" (Rev. 3:5). If you choose to be part of God's family, your name will remain in the Book of Life. If you do not, it will be blotted out. He chose you in Him before the foundation of the world. It is up to you to choose Him now in order to enjoy the eternal life He has provided.

In the Father's Heart

Having purposed to fulfill His dream for a family in spite of the cost, God began to unfold His eternal purpose by cutting an eon in half and calling it *time.* He began His work of creation and set mankind in the Garden of Eden. There He fellowshiped with the first ones He created to become the family that would satisfy His heart of love and fulfill His dream. But Adam and his wife failed the love test through their disobedience. The Voice came walking, seeking him. "Adam... 'Where are you?'" (Gen. 3:9, NKJV). Still the Father's purpose, known only to the Godhead, was not revealed to man. God couldn't tell Adam of the covenant of the Godhead because of his disobedience.

Centuries later, Moses received the Law of God, but that Law could not tell us what God's purpose was. That which was in God's heart—His dream—was not revealed. The historians, psalmists and poets of the Bible did not perceive it. Even the prophets were not aware of God's dream. Four hundred dark years after the prophets were silent, what God had planned was not yet revealed.

So God cut out His love in the form of a Person and sent Him to earth as the express image of God. Everything Jesus did, each word He spoke, was to show us the Father's heart. Jesus healed the sick and set the captives free to reveal to us the Father's love.

But almost no one got the message that Jesus was revealing God the Father to us. Just before Jesus left this earth, one of His disciples even asked Him, "Lord, show us the Father, and it is sufficient for us" (John 14:8, NKJV). We can almost hear the disappointment in Jesus' answer to His disciples: "Have I been so long time with you, and yet hast thou not known me...? He that hath seen me hath seen the Father" (v. 9).

Not even Jesus could tell His disciples what was in the Father's heart. They had centered their thoughts on the present earthly kingdom. Jesus said to them, "I have yet many things to say unto you, but ye cannot bear them now" (John 16:12). He told them He was returning to the Father so that the Counselor could come. The Holy Spirit was part of the plan; He was not an afterthought. He would move inside them and enlighten their minds. "When He, the Spirit of truth, has come, He will guide you into all truth…He will take of what is Mine and declare it to you" (John 16:13–14, NKJV).

Jesus completed the plan for redemption of mankind through His sacrifice on Calvary. The Holy Spirit was then entrusted to do His precious work in the earth to draw men to God. His task was to put into us what Jesus brought—that heartbeat. The throb of God's heart was still to have a family in His image, with His family spirit—the Spirit of the Lamb—to live and rule with Him. However, no one had yet been able to declare that purpose fully to us. On the Day of Pentecost, when the Holy Spirit came, Peter put his telescope to the entire church age, but he didn't see the whole purpose of God. He saw bits of its beginning and ending as he prophesied, but he didn't say a word about what was in the Father's heart. (See Acts 2.)

Then one day, a man with a slaughtering spirit, seemingly further from the heart of God than anyone could be, had a supernatural encounter with the living God and was apprehended for a special purpose. Saul of Tarsus was converted and became the apostle Paul. He was a "full gospel preacher" for a while, until God told him to go to the desert of Arabia. Without conferring with flesh and blood, he obeyed the Spirit's command. During the three years Paul spent in that desert, the Father unfolded to him the mystery that had been hidden since before the foundation of the world.

Paul explained to the church at Ephesus that God's

eternal purpose was "to make plain to everyone the administration of this mystery, which for ages past was kept hidden in God...His intent was that now, through the church, the manifold wisdom of God should be made known to the rulers and authorities in the heavenly realms, according to his eternal purpose which he accomplished in Christ Jesus our Lord" (Eph. 3:9–11, NIV). God was going to fulfill His purpose and realize His dream for a family through the church, the body of Christ on the earth.

Throughout Paul's christological epistles, he reveals the purpose of God for the church. God will have a glorious church that will bear His image, with each Christian fulfilling his purpose to be a part of forming the family that God desires. Paul declared:

> Speaking the truth in love, we will in all things grow up into him who is the Head, that is, Christ. From him the whole body, joined and held together by every supporting ligament, grows and builds itself up in love, as each part does its work.
>
> —EPHESIANS 4:15–16, NIV

It seems almost too good to be true that God will have a family as described by Paul, especially when we are living in homes and churches that seem to be full of "spots and wrinkles." Why is there such a disparity between what God intends for His family and who we are now? Where is the unity, the love, the Christlike humility that is to characterize the church? The answers to these questions will help us to close the gap between God's dream for a family that will reflect His nature and the people that we are today. We must believe that God's purpose will be fulfilled as He purposed it from eternity. He has promised:

> I will put my laws in their minds and write them on their hearts. I will be their God, and they will be my people. No longer will a man teach his neighbor, or a man his brother, saying, "Know the Lord," because they will all know me, from the least of them to the greatest.
>
> —HEBREWS 8:10–11, NIV

If you pursue the truth about yourself and allow the Holy Spirit to set you free from those characteristics and flaws of your sinful nature that keep you from reflecting the nature of Christ in your life, you will become part of fulfilling God's purpose in the earth.

When we were made, we were neither moral nor immoral, but were created amoral. We had to make a choice. God knew before He made us that man would fail the test of love and make the wrong choice. He also knew that if He sent His love and placed it within us, He could give us the family spirit of God. We cannot get that *family* spirit from anyone else.

Reality tells us that we are not born in the image of God as in the original Creation. We still have the potential for that image—we still have a spirit. However, our human spirit is dead because of Adam's sin. We have a soul made up of a mind, a will and emotions. The Bible says our minds are carnal, and our wills are rebellious (Rom. 8:7; Isa. 53:6). Did you ever hear a baby say *yes* before he said *no*? Experience tells us that our emotions are self-centered and warped. We concern ourselves more with how we are offended than we do with how we offend. All these human traits are contrary to the family spirit of God. So our spirits need to be made alive to God, and our souls need to be redeemed. We were created in the image of God, but we lost that image through Adam's disobedience.

Through disobedience God's purpose was thwarted. You cannot be in love with God without walking in obedience to Him. Jesus said, "If ye love me, keep my commandments" (John 14:15).

What helped me to learn to obey God was learning to love and to obey my daddy. His love for me motivated me. For example, he instilled in me the beauty of being virtuous, to the extent that if a boy had insulted me, I would have slapped him. My daddy inspired me by telling me how proud he was going to be to see me walk down the aisle as a virtuous young bride. I never went on a date without thinking about my daddy's advice. I had a little taste of what motivating love is—to do my daddy's will.

A baby doesn't know who his daddy is. All he knows is his daddy's provision. As a child grows up, there comes a time when he loves to obey his daddy. He begins to know him and to ask how he can help him, becoming more involved in his interests. The heavenly Father wants us to know Him as our Father. His whole purpose is that we might love Him, and prove that love through our obedience to Him.

OBEDIENCE REQUIRES A CROSS

If you are to come into obedience to the commands of God, you have to be willing to suffer. Because our natures are contrary to the nature of God, the process of becoming like Him will cause suffering to our souls.

When His will crosses ours, we begin to understand what it means to deny ourselves, take up the cross and follow Him. You must choose to give up your *ways*, your *will*, your *work*, your *walk*, your *words*, your *worship* and your *warfare*. You must be willing to exchange your sinful nature for the nature of God. This process of being changed into His image requires the work of the cross in each of our lives, daily allowing the Holy Spirit to change us.

In Moses' tabernacle, which is a type of our "temple," the furniture was laid out in the shape of a cross. It speaks of the cost of redemption and of what the Father suffered to change us into His image. Everything God made that has breath has a cross displayed in it. My face has a cross in it; my body forms a cross. Love came by way of the cross. We will experience the work of the cross in our lives if we respond in obedience to His love.

Many Charismatic teachers deny the need for suffering. They have taught us to rebuke everything the cross brought, to confess that we don't have to have anything that hurts or cuts away our self lives. They don't want to talk about the fourth baptism. We speak eagerly of the baptism into the body of Christ, water baptism, and the baptism in the Holy Spirit. The fourth baptism, baptism of suffering, however, is not as readily taught. We don't want to suffer.

We love to sing the words of the hymn, "At the cross, at the cross, where I first saw the light."[1] However, our position now is not "at" the cross. After we have seen the light, we change positions. Home becomes "in" the cross. Paul said, "God forbid that I should glory, save *in* the cross of our Lord Jesus Christ" (Gal. 6:14, emphasis added). <u>There is no way home without allowing the cross to destroy the self life so that we can receive the family spirit of God.</u>

Too often we find ourselves exalting the self life. When man is lacking the principles of true revelation, he will seek only that love that benefits him. Much of our preaching has emphasized what God can give us. In receiving salvation, we understand that Jesus saves us from sin and from hell. But we need to know more about God than just receiving His benefits. The Spirit reveals to the creature in Christ that God's *being* is preeminent over His *doing*. Who He is is more significant that what He does. What He does is for the purpose of our seeing who He is.

Do you measure your love for Him by what He does for you? If you do, then you are not involved in who He is. God is love, and as we have seen, that love involves suffering. Jesus said, "Anyone who does not take his cross and follow me is not worthy of me. Whoever finds his life will lose it, and whoever loses his life for my sake will find it" (Matt. 10:38–39, NIV). He promised us that a cross was involved in our knowing His love, but said that was the way to find life.

Jesus' love for us eventually led Him to Calvary. Where do we think our love for Him will lead us? As you lay down your selfish desires and allow God's love to be reflected in your nature, the world will see your love for God and for others. Then they will believe in Jesus. (See John 17:21.) This is my opinion, but I don't think we are going to demonstrate much of God's love until we experience some hurt-love. We are not God, but He is our Father. If we are to reflect His nature, then we must know the love that came out of pain—a love that suffered supreme cost. It is an unselfish love that loves at any price. Paul cried, "That I may know him, and the power of his resurrection, and the fellowship of his sufferings" (Phil. 3:10). He understood that suffering was an integral part of knowing God's love.

How can we experience that love if we are not willing to take up our own cross? How will we go home with His kind of hurt-love without experiencing death to the self life? Jesus suffered the loss of everything He had in the Godhead to bring His love to us. Yet we aren't willing to suffer a little crucifixion of our selfish desires, but would rather preach "self-esteem" and "my rights." That is not the heartbeat of God or His nature.

One of the six requirements Jesus laid down for discipleship is that you love Him above everything else. That requires allowing the cross to destroy your love of self. Walking in obedience to the commands of God, you must deny the sinful propensities in your will, mind and emotions. That is how you bear the cross daily, just as Jesus instructed us to do. The Holy Spirit changes your decisions, thoughts and desires, causing you to fulfill God's pleasure in your life. What you take to the cross in death will come forth in life on the other side of the cross. You demonstrate that life in your love for God, which is reflected in your obedience to Him.

There is an earnest cry being born in many hearts to know who God is. I believe the next move of God is going to unveil the heavenly Father as we have never known Him. Who is your Father? He is love. You must respond to His hurt-love by being willing to carry your cross and lose your self life, to become conformed to His image. Can you imagine the joy of the Father when He sees the family come home as He dreamed? His very heartbeat expressed the desire to have a family in His image, with His Spirit and His nature, one that loves Him with His kind of love: *hurt-love.*

God's eternal purpose will be realized in your individual life, in your home and, ultimately, in the church as you are conformed to the image of Christ through the working of the Holy Spirit in you. If you are to fully understand God's purpose for you, you will need to cultivate a relationship with the Holy Spirit. Learn to understand who He is. Cooperate with Him as He works to fulfill God's purpose for mankind.

---

1. "At the Cross" by Isaac Watts. Public domain.

Chapter 2

GOD'S PURPOSE
CONFIRMED

When Jesus told His disciples that He would return to the Father and send the Holy Spirit to teach them all things, He was actually revealing the next step in the fulfillment of God's purpose (John 14:26). The Holy Spirit had been entrusted with the task of ultimately bringing the family of God home, changed into the image of God. In eternity, this Third Person of God had suffered His *kenosis* and had chosen to become a servant to do His part to bring a family back to the Father.

There have been many outpourings of the Holy Spirit since the Day of Pentecost as the Servant has been faithful in His part of fulfilling God's eternal purpose. In every move of God, the Holy Spirit has restored truths to the church and empowered men and women to declare the gospel in a way that has resulted in great ingatherings of souls. However, I believe there is coming an outpouring of the Holy Spirit such as we have never seen before. If you meet the conditions, you are going to be a part of the fulfillment of God's Word, which promises that "the earth will be filled with the knowledge of the glory of the LORD, as the waters cover the sea" (Hab. 2:14, NIV).

In 1963, while I was ministering in a church in Klamuth Falls, Oregon, the Lord spoke to me, saying that if I would stay in His Presence, He would show me what was going to happen in the church and what He was going to do in the world when He poured out His revival. So I waited there in prayer, and He took me into the heavenlies and let me see the revival that is coming. I saw it more clearly than I see the faces of men.

The Holy Spirit used the analogy of a hydroelectric power plant to explain to me what He was doing. (I knew nothing about electricity—I couldn't have fixed a light switch if my life depended upon it.) Hour after hour He carried me in the heavenlies, showing me heaven's *dunamis*. In the heavens above the church, God was doing the excavation for the building of a huge power plant. I saw how carefully He laid the foundation and how exactly He measured the sand that went into it. He cleansed everything and placed every screen and tube in order precisely as they should be. Then He ran the prime lines, the primary lines and the secondary lines out through transformers.

As I watched, I saw that the power came down through the church. Jesus is the Head of the church, and He was holding this gigantic power plant in His hands. From the church His power flowed throughout the entire world. I saw five geographical locations in the United States where there would be vital hubs. In these areas, God would dig many deep reservoirs, connecting pipes together, as "deep calleth unto deep" (Ps. 42:7). The Holy Spirit was creating a network of churches. He would dig out these deep reservoirs, and then He would pour His Spirit into them, creating fountains out of which would flow living water. "Deep" would call to another "deep" until there was a great network of churches filled with living water.

When everything was in order, I saw that He was going to pull a great switch and send an "old-fashioned, heaven-sent, sky-blue, sin-killing, gully-washing" revival. Then I heard the water begin to run. I knew the water was the Word, and I saw churches as reservoirs, filling up with water, getting ready for Him to pull the switch. When God releases that *dunamis*, His power, out of our innermost being will flow "rivers of living water" (John 7:38). "The earth shall be full of the knowledge of the LORD, as the waters cover the sea" (Isa. 11:9).

The Greek word for *Holy Spirit* is *dunamis*, from which we derive our word *dynamo*. The analogy of a power plant was a descriptive word picture to reveal the workings of our heavenly *Dunamis*.

My Father said to me, "I am running the pipes now." With my natural ear, I heard the water roll into those pipes from October to December of that year. Finally I prayed, "Father, if it please You, turn the water sound inside, but let me continue to hear it." I have been to churches where I have heard the sound of those waters, confirming to me that they are reservoirs to be connected with the network of pipes. The Lord said to me, "This time when I pull that great power switch, no demon, devil, man or denomination will ever dam it up again, and many souls are going to be won. I will do a quick work; I am going to bring a revival that will reach the world."

In that vision, God let me see the ministry of the local

church. I understood that as the church, we would take care of the elderly and feed the poor, train disciples and teach ministers, raising them up to possess the land. I saw the printed page rolling, and I watched the church walk into the heavenlies and take the powers of the media away from the devil. (After receiving this vision, I went through the country preaching what God had spoken to me, and people looked at me as if to say, "Poor thing, she is getting old.") I saw the grain fields of the world ready to be harvested, and my Father said it was going to happen soon. Since then I have stood on the shores of the isles of the sea in Trinidad and the Bahamas and heard that water running. God gave me that vision over thirty-five years ago, and I believe we are that much closer to fulfilling our Father's dream.

PREREQUISITE FOR REVIVAL

There are conditions to be met if we expect to be part of this coming revival. The power of the Holy Spirit will only flow through those who have been prepared to be His vessels. Much of what I had seen in that vision related directly to the preparation of God's people for the coming revival.

Several years ago when I was still pastoring in Dallas, Texas, while I was waiting on God before ministering on a Sunday to my congregation, my Father brought something to my attention that shook me. My heart was tuned to what the Lord wanted to say to the congregation that morning. As I waited before the Lord, He spoke a word that dramatically influenced my leaving that pastorate and has shaped my preaching since that time. He said that revival was not coming to

America *unless* and *until* the church becomes more *personally* and *intimately acquainted* with the Third Person of the Godhead.

Knowing the Holy Spirit Intimately

We must become more sensitive to the Holy Spirit and learn to cooperate with Him, or revival will not come to this nation. When He spoke of His church, He wasn't talking about an institution, a denomination or a building. He was referring to the living organism, His body, which includes every person who has been born of His Spirit. The Father deliberately referred to the Third Person of the Godhead, rather than to the Holy Spirit, because He is intent in His purpose that we know the Holy Spirit as God.

"Father, are You saying the Charismatic church does not know the Third Person of the Godhead intimately, does not cooperate with Him and is not sensitive to Him?" I protested. I wept that night when He told me we are holding back the deluge of blessing that God intends us to have because we don't know the blessed Holy Spirit as we need to. With tears running down my cheeks, I cried, "My Father, ever since 1959 when You healed me and filled me with Your Holy Spirit, I have tried to walk in the Spirit. Please tell me what is wrong. What are You saying, Father, that I don't understand? Why don't we know this Third Person of the Godhead?"

A misinterpretation of the Scriptures

The first reason He gave for our lack of relationship with the Holy Spirit was a *misinterpretation of the Scriptures.* That disturbed me, since I had spent seventeen years attempting to be an exegetical, systematic theology professor, rightly dividing the Word of God. He could not have spoken a more serious indictment to me than that I was not interpreting His Word correctly. However, He directed my attention to John 16:13: "Howbeit when he, the Spirit of truth, is come, he will guide you into all truth: for he shall not speak of himself; but whatsoever he shall hear, that shall he speak: and he will shew you things to come." Then He showed me that the church has taken the little preposition *of* in the phrase "he shall not speak *of* himself," and interpreted it to mean that He does not speak *about* Himself. I had to admit that I have interpreted this Scripture in that way.

The Father asked me, "Why do you like to read the red letters in your Bible?"

I replied, "Because they are the words of my Lord."

He reminded me that Jesus did not say they were His words. Jesus said, "And the word which ye hear is not mine, but the Father's which sent me" (John 14:24). Jesus spoke what He heard His Father speaking. When Jesus said of Himself, "I am the way, the truth, and the life" (John 14:6), He was teaching us about Himself, though the source of revelation was the Father. In the same way, the Holy Spirit speaks about Himself, for the Scriptures tell us that the Holy Spirit wrote the Book. "For the prophecy came not in old time by the will of man: but holy men of God spake as they were moved by the Holy Ghost" (2 Pet. 1:21). Since the Holy Spirit wrote the Scriptures, and there are over two hundred verses in the New Testament that tell us who He is, we must understand that the Holy Spirit speaks about Himself.

What, then, did Jesus mean when He said that the
Holy Spirit will not speak *of* Himself? He meant that
the Holy Spirit didn't speak *out of His own resources*, but
was speaking what the Father gave Him to speak, just as
Jesus did. The Father made me to understand that what
we have taught in the church about the Holy Spirit has
given the impression that we should not inquire to
know Him as a Person. We have taught that He doesn't
speak about Himself because of His humility, and that
His task is only to reveal Jesus to us. So we refer to the
Holy Spirit as "it" or "tongues" or "gifts." Every Bible
school I know of that includes a class on pneumatology
studies "spiritual gifts" rather than the Person of the
Holy Ghost. We have studied His gifts, not His Person.
He is the Third Person of the Godhead; we need to
become acquainted with Him personally.

A point of reference

The second reason we don't know the Holy Spirit
intimately is because we don't have a *point of reference*
for relating to Him. We understand the idea of a heavenly Father in relation to how we understand our relationships with our earthly fathers. I can say "Father,"
and relate to God somewhat as I related to my own
daddy. My papa was perhaps the godliest person I have
ever known, a man of sterling character. I am a minister of the Lord because my daddy taught me to love and
obey him. Though I didn't always want to obey, my
daddy didn't excuse my disobedience by saying, "She is
just a child." He taught me that his word was to be
obeyed, and he set up specific guidelines for me. I had
no problems if I obeyed them, but if I didn't, I would
suffer the consequences. I learned that my daddy meant

exactly what he said, which gave me a good understanding of how to respond to God's commands. My father was not just a man of his word, however. He was also my dearest friend in whom I could confide when I couldn't go to anyone else.

When relating to my heavenly Father, I can simply enlarge upon my understanding of my earthly father. I don't have any problem crawling up in my heavenly Father's lap and saying, "Put Your arms around me, Daddy; Your daughter would like to talk to You." When I don't understand something, I just say, "Father, I don't understand that. Will You talk to me about it?" I expect Him to talk to me because of the way my daddy talked to me. I believed what my daddy said. If there is one thing on earth that my daddy would never have done, it was to tell me a lie. For that reason, I can easily go to my heavenly Father and know that He is truthful. So the night my heavenly Father called me into the ministry, I did not consider disobeying my "Daddy." Though I had never seen a female preacher, I believed God when He told me He wanted me to preach. And when my Father talks to me about what is going to take place in the days ahead, I believe it with all my heart and am preparing for it. In this way, our relationship to our earthly father becomes a point of reference for helping us to relate to a heavenly Father.

When we think of Jesus, the Son of God, we are able to imagine the kind of person He was when He walked the streets of Jerusalem. Each of us has an image in our mind of Jesus when He was on earth. He was limited to a human body that probably weighed less than two hundred pounds and was less than six feet tall. He never traveled over twenty miles in one day, never wrote a book, never preached on radio or TV. He blessed children and healed the sick. His church consisted of twelve members, and one of them became a traitor. As we describe Jesus' life on this earth, we confirm our point of reference to His Person.

However, when we think of the Holy Spirit, we don't have any point of reference to understand His Person. He is a Person, just as the Father and the Son are Persons. He has taken up His residence in the church, which is the body of Christ. Each of us is a temple of the Holy Spirit. We can see the beauty of God in each other because the Holy Spirit lives in us. When I see faces shining, I know the Holy Spirit is in those lives. His glory is in the temple. Although this reality is somewhat abstract to grasp, you can learn to appreciate the beauty of God in your brothers and sisters as you see the Holy Spirit in their lives.

The emblems and gifts of the Spirit

A third reason we do not know the Holy Spirit as a Person is because we have difficulty with corporeality, that which is not physical. Therefore, we try to relate to Him through the *emblems* that represent Him and through the *gifts* He bestows. We substitute fourteen emblems to represent Him, and we say that they are the Holy Spirit. For example, we say the Holy Spirit is "the wind." He is not the wind, though He manifests Himself in that way sometimes. Similarly, we call Him "a dove." He has never been a dove, though He has used doves to manifest His presence. Sometimes we refer to the oil of the Spirit, but the Holy Spirit is not oil. He is a Person, the Third Person of the Godhead.

During the Charismatic movement, we gave much of our attention to the gifts of the Holy Spirit. The Father sent the Holy Spirit to the church with twenty-one gifts to help us on our homeward journey. However, we see His gifts and call them the Holy Spirit. Abraham sent his servant with gifts to find a wife for Isaac. The gifts were only to help them talk about Isaac until she arrived at her new home. The servant, representing the Holy Spirit in type, became her companion on the long journey home to find her bridegroom. The closer to her new home Rebekah came, the less she noticed gifts, and the more she looked for Isaac. When she saw him vaguely in sight, she asked if it was Isaac in the shadows, and the servant told her it was. She was no longer involved in gifts, but was putting on a veil to get ready for the wedding. She had found her way to her bridegroom, not because of gifts she had received, but because of the servant companion who had led her home.

Because of a misinterpretation of Scripture, we have de-emphasized the Holy Spirit's place as God. And because of our difficulty within corporeality, in that we have no point of reference, along with an overemphasis on spiritual gifts, we have not given due regard to know the Holy Spirit as a Person. Some have stooped, and I feel it is an abomination, to refer to Him as *it*. We need to respect Him as the Third Person of God, who dwells in every believer. "Know ye not that your body is the temple of the Holy Ghost which is in you?" (1 Cor. 6:19). He is the Third Person of God who lives in the hearts of born-again believers, His church.

What Is a Person?

What constitutes a person? Inside each of us there is an inner sanctuary called our *spirit*. The human spirit is a vacuum, created in a shape that only the residence of Almighty God can fill. No other person is able to fulfill the need of your spirit, for you were created for God's presence. Surrounding that spirit, there is a soul that consists of your will (or volition), your mind and your emotions. Your spirit and your soul are contained in your physical *body*, which makes every person a triune being made up of spirit, soul and body.

When we think of the Holy Spirit as a Person, we must understand that He has a will, He has a mind, and He has emotions. We are to become His body to express the will of God in the church. "And he who searches our hearts knows the mind of the Spirit, because the Spirit intercedes for the saints in accordance with God's will" (Rom. 8:27). The Holy Spirit acts in harmony with the *will* of God, praying through you according to His will. He knows the *mind* of God and wants to communicate that understanding to you so that your thoughts can become His thoughts. He also expresses emotion as a Person.

The Holy Spirit has emotions that He wants to express through His people in praise, celebration, worship and prayer. He is a Person who desires to dwell in believers, giving them the mind of God, doing the will of God and expressing godly emotions.

As you yield to the work of the Holy Spirit within you, you are cultivating a relationship with Him that will allow you to be a part of fulfilling God's dream for a family that bears His image. You will learn to become more sensitive to His will and purposes and to cooperate with Him in His task of preparing a family for the Father. The Third Person of God wants to indwell believers in a way that will bring you into perfect harmony with the purposes of God for your individual life, your home and your church.

Chapter 3

CULTIVATING GOD'S PURPOSE

Cultivating a relationship with the Holy Spirit requires yielding to Him at every point where your will, your thoughts and your desires differ with His divine purpose. The Holy Spirit comes to dwell in your spirit, filling you with the life of God. He must express that life, however, through your soul. God's will must become your will, His thoughts your thoughts and His desires your desires expressed through your actions, your mind and your emotions.

In Moses' tabernacle there was a veil between the holy of holies and the holy place that hid the presence of God from the view of the people. Only the priest could go behind that veil, and then only once a year to atone for the sins of the people. Scripture teaches that, as Christians, we are tabernacles of God. The presence of God dwells in the spirits of born-again believers. Most of us have Jesus "locked up" behind a veil in our spirits. I treated Him that way for seventeen years as an old-fashioned, holiness-taught Methodist preacher. Jesus was locked in my spirit, just as He was hidden from view behind the veil in Moses' tabernacle.

I didn't know that I had Jesus locked behind the veil

inside. I shouted joyfully when I understood that the veil of the temple that had separated man from God's presence was rent asunder that day at Calvary. I rejoiced because the opening of that veil signified that I personally could go into God's presence. However, I did not realize that the veil of flesh in my soul kept the Spirit of God from filling my temple. When God sent the Holy Spirit to earth to dwell in your spirit and to make you His temple, He planned to rip open that veil of flesh and allow Jesus to fill your entire sanctuary. His intent was to make your mind become His mind, your will His will, your emotions His emotions. The Holy Spirit would fill your temple—and the temple of each believer—with His glory. This glory is not an essence to be seen floating in the shape of a cloud, but is rather the presence of God manifest in our lives and filling the church.

When we ask the Person of the Holy Spirit to take His abode inside us, we surrender our all to Him. That being the case, I have a few questions to ask. Can you articulate what He has taught you this week? He is the Teacher. Do you know what the offices of the Holy Spirit are? How many of them has He fulfilled in you this week? Do you know His voice? Do you recognize His classroom? Did you ever ask Him why He came or what His mandate is?[1]

YIELDING TO GOD'S SPIRIT

He can't fulfill His mandate without dwelling in us, yet the people in whom He lives generally know very little about Him. If you have told the Holy Ghost that your life is His home, when He comes into your life and finds things foreign to Him, He will follow His mandate to clean you, change you and fill you full of the Godhead. He comes to teach you because He knows you are ignorant. He comes to clean you because He knows you are dirty. He comes to give you life because He knows you are dead. This is the only way you will ever be changed into the image of your Father. The Holy Spirit makes the Bible come alive, places that life inside you and changes your nature, replacing Adam's fallen nature with Christ's divine nature.

The Holy Spirit will often bring something to your attention and ask, "Is this yours?"

Do you look at it and say, "No, it is my husband's"? Do you excuse yourself by saying that you got it from mama or that you are the victim of child abuse? It seems today that everyone is a victim of something. In reality, we are all victims of sin. We don't need to be petted and pampered or justified for who we are. We need to be forgiven. Then we must allow God to heal us, free us and change us into His image through our yielding to the Holy Spirit daily.

One of the ways we yield to the Holy Spirit is to praise and worship God. In the Scriptures, when we get a glimpse of life in heaven, we always see worship happening around the throne of God. The Holy Spirit enters the sanctuary of our spirits and sets our lives in harmony with the throne of God through worship.

Another way we yield to the Holy Spirit is by allowing Him to pray through us. There is a clearer teaching about prayer coming to the church now. We are learning not to bring our want lists to the Father because we don't know what we need. There is Someone else in us who prays according to the will of God for us. As Paul declared:

> Likewise the Spirit also helpeth our infirmities: for we know not what we should pray for as we ought: but the Spirit itself maketh intercession for us with groanings which cannot be uttered. And he that searcheth the hearts knoweth what is the mind of the Spirit, because he maketh intercession for the saints according to the will of God.
>
> —Romans 8:26–27

If you don't experience His intercessions, you cannot claim the next verse, which promises, "And we know that all things work together for good to them that love God, to them who are the called according to his purpose" (Rom. 8:28). The Godhead is working out the Father's purpose in your heart. The Holy Spirit prays according to what is in the Father's heart, because He was in on the covenant before the foundation of the world. All things work together for good to those who love God and are called according to His eternal plan, His purpose. Because we don't know what is in the Father's heart, we don't know how to pray as we ought; but the Teacher does. So He comes to teach you to pray according to His will, which, ultimately, is to make you like Christ. "For whom he did foreknow, he also did predestinate to be conformed to the image of his Son, that he might be the firstborn among many brethren" (Rom. 8:29). Allowing the Holy Spirit to pray through you is an important part of your being conformed to His image.

Besides yielding to the Holy Spirit in praise and

worship and allowing Him to pray through you, you
must also allow Him to cleanse you in order that
you might bear the family spirit in the image of God.
Be careful not to fail in your cooperation with the Holy
Spirit at this point. Don't resist His convicting power
when it points to your need for change. Some will take
delight in His speaking in His languages and bringing
gifts and power, but they want Him to go no further
because the Word tells us that when He comes, He
brings with Him a broom, a fan, a fire and fullers' soap.
He is expecting to clean up something that is dirty.
Adam, with his self life, has lived there and been in
control long enough.

Give control of your life to the Holy Spirit, even
though you know very little about Him. He came to
change your nature and to unveil the nature of Jesus in
you. Though He speaks in heavenly languages and
gives gifts, that is not the reason He came. His mandate
is to unveil the Christ who lives in you until you know
Him intimately as your Bridegroom and reflect His
image in your life. His purpose is to bring life to the
written Word until it becomes the living Christ to you,
living His life through you.

Paul declares that it is "Christ in you, the hope of
glory" (Col. 1:27). One day Christ will fill your temple
with His glory. No one can make that happen except
the Holy Spirit. He came to split the veil of flesh open
and to let Christ out of your spirit to fill your mind,
your will and your emotions. He came to quicken your
mortal body as well (Rom. 8:11).

This understanding of "Christ in you" does not deny
the reality of the literal Person of Jesus. Jesus is our

High Priest who "ever liveth to make intercession for [us]" (Heb. 7:25). He invited Thomas to feel the scars of His hands and side. Those scars are still there, and that body now "appear[s] in the presence of God for us" (Heb. 9:24). We are looking for Jesus to appear again, so that our decaying bodies can be changed and "fashioned like unto his glorious body" (Phil. 3:21). That is the hope of the church. However, the work of the Holy Spirit is to reveal the nature of Jesus in us. I was not born with the mind of God, the will of God or the emotions of God. My soul was warped. So when the Holy Ghost moved into my spirit, He wanted to possess my temple.

As long as you are in control, He can't be. The "I" nature wants to rule, having your own way and exercising your rights, never allowing the Holy Spirit to do what He came to do. If you take your "I" to the cross, you can exchange it there for the I AM. Then the Holy Spirit moves into every area of your personality and the veil of flesh begins to fall away. You will begin to realize that you don't think as you used to think. The truth will dawn on you: "These aren't my thoughts." Then you will understand Paul's injunction: "Let this mind be in you, which was also in Christ Jesus" (Phil. 2:5). He also admonishes, "Whatsoever things are true, whatsoever things are honest, whatsoever things are just, whatsoever things are pure, whatsoever things are lovely, whatsoever things are of good report…think on these things" (Phil. 4:8).

The Holy Spirit begins to replace Adam's carnal mind with the mind of Christ so you can think like your Daddy thinks. Then He changes your rebellious

will as well. As you keep surrendering to the Holy
Spirit, He begins to take the Father's will, which we
know nothing about, and moves into your will. He
makes your will His will, and His will your will. You
don't have to pray in fear, wondering if you are doing
what He wants. As you yield to the Holy Spirit's work
within you, you begin to walk with God and to become
the will of God.

In the same way, your emotions need to be changed
by the Holy Spirit. Some of us may declare, "I am not
emotional."

God says, "I know, that is why I have to 'work you
over.'" Your emotions constitute one-third of your
soul. If you do not express His emotions, that area of
your personality is dead. When the Holy Spirit moves
into your temple, He comes to set your house in order,
not just for eternity, but so you can live now as well.
Then you can say with Paul, "I am crucified with
Christ: nevertheless I live: yet not I, but Christ liveth in
me: and the life which I now live in the flesh I live by
the faith of the Son of God, who loved me, and gave
himself for me" (Gal. 2:20).

A Testimony

No doubt I would be dead today were it not for a little
preacher who had yielded himself to the Holy Spirit.
He had learned to be sensitive to Him and to cooperate with Him. We had already had six deaths in our
family, including those of my two brothers and my
father. Just a few months earlier, an ambulance had
carried me from a hospital in Greensboro, North
Carolina, to my daddy's funeral. The nurses packed me

carefully onto a stretcher so that my backbone would not vibrate, causing it to break into pieces. It seemed I was to be the next to join those of my family who had preceded me in death. I had resigned from my pastorate and from the college where I had taught, had chosen my pallbearers and had listened to the trumpeter who was to play at my funeral.

At the cemetery where my daddy was being buried, I asked the undertaker not to lower his casket into the hole until I left. We had buried five other members of my family, and I had heard "ashes to ashes" all I wanted to hear it. So I asked them to leave him on the green mound. As my ambulance pulled away from that cemetery, I waved back at the green mound and said, "I will join you, Daddy, in a few months."

A few weeks earlier, when my father was ill, he had walked out of his room with his Bible in his hand, and he said to me, "Pastor, I think we have missed something." (I had been his pastor for nine years.)

I replied, "What have we missed, Papa?"

He said, "I think we have missed knowing the God of Elijah. Elijah could lay his body on people, and they were healed." With tears in his eyes, he asked, "Why is our family dying?"

I told him what I had been taught. I said, "Daddy, we don't need that now. Healing is not for us today. That which is perfect has come. We have the Word. The Word is that which is perfect."

As he left the room, he said to me, "I still believe the God of Elijah is alive." That was my last conversation with my father about the Word before His death.

A few months after my daddy's death, during which

time I was admitted to two different North Carolina hospitals, I was carried into a church on a Sunday morning, one I had not been in before. I was expecting that service to perhaps be the last I would ever attend. The man who was to preach was not the pastor of the church. He was the former pastor who was now a superintendent, but he had been invited to speak on that particular Sunday. He was over seventy years old, and he knew God. *He knew the Holy Spirit.* He arrived on Saturday and was staying in a hotel, preparing to speak the following morning.

At four o'clock on Sunday morning, the Holy Spirit awakened him and instructed him to preach a sermon titled, "Where Is the Lord God of Elijah?" He reminded the Lord that he had already preached that sermon to this church when he was pastoring there. The Lord replied, "I know that; I keep the records." God simply requested him to preach what He asked him to preach. In obedience to the Spirit of God, he preached about the God of Elijah, not knowing I would be present in that congregation. He could not have known of the conversation about Elijah that I had with my daddy. He simply followed the mind of the Spirit and set the stage for what caught my attention—the "faith of Elijah." If he had preached about speaking in tongues, I would not have been listening. As a Methodist professor, my theology would not have accepted it. I was a born-again, prayed-up, paid-up, packed-up woman ready to go up, but I didn't believe in healing or speaking in tongues.

That little man did one of the most unusual things I had ever seen. As he was preaching, he declared, "If you had the faith of Elijah, you could see what Elijah saw." Then he stepped beside the pulpit, looked me straight in the eye and said, "My beloved, you may have followed behind the dearest one on earth to you and left him on a *green mound,* but he wants you to know that he did not take his God away from you. The God of Elijah is in this church today."

At that moment, the God of Elijah nudged me to go forward for prayer. I responded, "They are not having an altar call." In a few moments, we began to sing an old Methodist hymn. The words of the third stanza were: "He saw me plunged in deep distress and flew to my release."[2] When we began singing those words, the Holy Spirit spoke to me again, telling me to go forward in prayer. I asked the lady who had brought me to the church to stand me up.

Thinking I was suffering, she responded, "We will be leaving in a few minutes."

I repeated, "Stand me up." Later, she told me that the tone of my voice let her know she had better stand me up, which she hastened to do.

In the eyes of all those people, I did something that ordinarily would have made me feel totally out of order. I walked up, looked into that preacher's face and said, "Sir, I don't know why I am here. In obedience to God's prompting I have come. Maybe you should pray for me." He reached into the podium and brought out a vial of oil and "greased" me. After praying a simple prayer, he said, "In Jesus' name," in a way I had never heard it said before. I knew that man knew Him in a way I did not.

I thanked him and started dragging myself back to

my seat in my braces. What crossed my mind was that
I must have been anointed for my burial. When I
reached the seventh row, where I had been sitting, God
spoke to me in a thundering voice. I thought everyone
in the church heard it. He said, "If ye be willing and
obedient, ye shall eat the good of the land" (Isa. 1:19).
Standing there in my braces, I suddenly knew I was
going to live, though I thought I would remain crippled. God asked me if I was willing to be identified
with these Pentecostal people. I said, "Yes, sir."

Turning in my braces, I said to the preacher, "Sir,
may I give a testimony?" He replied that testimonies
were in order there. Hugging my Bible, with tears running down my cheeks, I said to that church, "Jesus has
just told me I am going to live. I believe I am going to
get to preach this Book yet. Even crippled for the rest
of my life, it would be wonderful to live to preach the
Word." When I had finished saying that and started
into my seat, the power of God struck the base of my
cranium. It traveled down my spine and came back up
to my head. One hour and twenty minutes later, I had
danced all over that church, right out of my braces, run
the aisle and exhausted every adjective I could find to
thank God for healing my body! (They told me later
there were three hundred people on the floor acting as
"bad" as I was acting.)

I shouted, "Bless the Lord, O my soul, and all that is
within me!" My soul obeyed me, and I heard a new
language come out of my mouth, one that I didn't
understand or believe in. I listened to the Electrician of
Eternity pick up the phone, dial heaven and say, "Give
heaven this new address of an earthly temple. I have

just moved in to set up worship and communion inside her and to cleanse this temple. I will set up My classroom and write the Word of God on the tablets of her heart." The Holy Spirit had invaded a Methodist minister's sanctuary. I spent the next five years trying to find out who this Third Person of God was. I searched the Scriptures to learn about the One whom I had thought I already knew.

THE HOLY SPIRIT IN THE CHURCH

I was grieved when God told me that the church doesn't know the Holy Spirit as we need to. I wept that night, vowing by the grace of God to do all I could to help people come to know the Holy Spirit. He came to set up the spirit of supplication and grace, of resurrection and life. He operates in seven different moods and manifests seven different powers through us. He is assigned sixty-six different functions in every one of us.[3] When we cooperate with Him, we become people who walk in the Spirit. Paul prayed for the church at Ephesus, "That the God of our Lord Jesus Christ, the Father of glory, may give unto you the spirit of wisdom and revelation in the knowledge of him: The eyes of your understanding being enlightened; that ye may know what is the hope of his calling, and what the riches of the glory of his inheritance in the saints" (Eph. 1:17–18). I had always thought that Paul prayed for the church at Ephesus that they would have the spirit of wisdom. However, the Holy Spirit prayed through Paul for the entire church, and His prayers will be answered. The church is going to have the spirit of wisdom to know who Jesus is. What is ahead is not just a little word of wisdom once in a while. The spirit of wisdom will settle on the church and open our spiritual eyes and ears until we can see and hear the truth of the Word of God.

We are going to be changed into His image and become the family of God by yielding to the work of the Holy Spirit in us. The Holy Spirit came to give us the family spirit because we have nothing like it. The family spirit is the Lamb spirit, the spirit of a servant. The very nature of the Third Person of God is the nature of a servant, doing the Father's bidding to give to us the life of Jesus and to present a family to the Father. As we come to know the Holy Spirit personally, we will undoubtedly find ourselves yielding to the call to servanthood.

---

1. For Dr. Pickett's complete study of the Holy Spirit, see *Presenting the Holy Spirit* (Lake Mary, FL: Charisma House, 1997).

2. "Majestic Sweetness Sits Enthroned" by Samuel Stennett. Public domain.

3. Pickett, *Presenting the Holy Spirit*.

Chapter 4

CALLED TO
GOD'S PURPOSE

I f you understand what God is saying today, then
you are hearing the call of the Holy Spirit for the
perfecting of His church. Everywhere I travel, I find
that those who are flowing in God's present moving
are preaching these same themes, which express
God's heart cry for His church today. This is an eightfold cry of the heart of the Lord.

The first of those themes is *repentance.* Repentance
must become a continuous process in our walk with
God, rather than something we do one time when we
receive Jesus as Savior. It is necessary that repentance
become a way of life for us so that we experience the
holiness God requires.

A second theme to which God is calling His church is
true *holiness,* which is perfected as our nature is
exchanged for God's nature. He is making us holy
because He is holy, and He is going to have a
holy church. God has also declared that His house shall
be "a house of prayer for all nations" (Isa. 56:7, NIV).

He is calling His church to *prayer.*

Revival is another of God's calls to His church today.
He is beginning even now to move in many churches in

a way that can only be identified as a cleansing move of God. It is just beginning, but many are testifying of Holy Ghost revival in their churches.

God's purposes include full *restoration* of the church and of the home to divine order. Unfortunately, the church world has taken the doctrine of fallen man and taught it as "divine order." God's intention, however, is to restore the home to His divine order.

Forgiveness must flow as well between brothers and sisters in the church to fulfill God's purposes. In her book *The Forgiving Church*, Sue Curran writes:

> Our churches maintain their vitality through the cleansing and release of forgiveness. The disease of unforgiveness threatens that life, for where the church fails to forgive, it ceases to live.[1]

The call to *worship* God in spirit and in truth is ringing loud and clear today. I believe God is calling the church to a higher dimension of worship than she has experienced before.

All these themes are timely messages of the Spirit of God to the church today, offering truth that can set us free to fulfill God's purpose for a family that bears His image.

THE CALL TO SERVANTHOOD

However, we are not hearing very much about one of the key calls of God to the church, without which it will be impossible to fulfill God's purpose. For God to realize His dream for a family, His children must respond to the call to *servanthood*—to becoming a servant. It is quite possible that our definition of success differs dramatically from God's idea of true greatness. Jesus told His disciples, "Whosoever will be great among you, let him be your minister; and whosoever will be chief among you, let him be your servant" (Matt. 20:26–27).

You must learn to value what God values and to esteem what He esteems. Perhaps the truth of servant-hood is not an exciting revelation, but without allowing it to become a reality in your life, you cannot hope to become part of fulfilling God's dream. Jesus "did not come to be served, but to serve" (Matt. 20:28, NIV). Scripture also portrays the Holy Spirit as a servant. Your attitude is to be the same as that of Jesus: "Who…made himself nothing, taking the very nature of a servant" (Phil. 2:7, NIV).

SERVANT BY CHOICE

The apostle Paul declared, "For though I be free from all men, yet have I made myself servant unto all, that I might gain the more" (1 Cor. 9:19). What Paul actually said was that he made himself a slave to serve everyone in order to bring them to an understanding of the gospel. What was Paul's perspective of servanthood? He was a Hebrew who was well acquainted with the Law. He knew that during the time of the Old Testament, slaves were freed every seventh year. When a slave was freed, he could choose to stay with his master. He would not be a bond slave any longer, but would become a love slave. If he chose to do that, he declared it publicly by laying his head on the doorpost and allowing someone to bore a hole in his ear. By placing an earring in his bored ear, he declared he was no longer a bond slave, but was by choice a love slave for the rest of his life. (See Exodus 21:1–6.)

For a long time I voiced a prayer and didn't really know what I was asking. I prayed, "Father, open my ears, and let me be where I can hear You." As I was studying the Word, I learned that to have your ear "digged" or opened means to have it "bored." The psalmist cried, "Mine ears hast thou opened" (Ps. 40:6). The opening of our ear to hear God's voice requires the process of having it bored, as was the ear of the love slave. We should not wonder why we cannot hear what God is saying to the church if we have not had our ear bored and become a love slave. That involves coming to the Father and declaring, "I am not serving You for promotion or position; I'm not serving You for pay or for profit, vacation or benefits. I'm serving You because I love the family spirit. I choose to be a love slave." When you say that you do not hear God speak to you, you are making an announcement affirming that you are not a servant.

A *doulos* is a love slave with a bored ear who, without hesitation, reservation or further information, does what the Master says. There is nothing in the love slave that wants to refuse. He never expects to choose another profession or seek another master. He serves because of love and because he wants to represent his master. This servant's only concern is that he recognizes the Master's voice. Jesus said, "My sheep hear my voice" (John 10:27).

THE MASTER'S CALL

God is faithful to speak to us about our responsibilities

in our relationship to Him and His promise of provision in His relationship to us. He has carefully clarified our "job description" as servants to let us know what He expects of us. As we fulfill the Scriptures regarding the call to servanthood, we can know we are pleasing Him and finding His favor.

One of the first things you must understand is that you are not a cochairman—you are a *colaborer with God*. The Scriptures declare that "we are labourers together with God" (1 Cor. 3:9). God is the unquestionable Chief from whom we receive all our instructions. Jesus challenges us to, "Take my yoke upon you, and learn of me" (Matt. 11:29). He is telling us to learn of His nature, for He is gentle and lowly of heart. Then we shall find rest for our souls, for His yoke is easy and His burden is light. To be a *yokefellow* simply means to work together as a teammate. Servanthood is the path of peace for all who will truly follow Christ.

As we choose to become colaborers with God in the path of servanthood, the Lord teaches us where our *source of strength* for service lies. "They that wait upon the Lord shall renew their strength" (Isa. 40:31). We know there is a waiting on God in prayer to receive His empowering. The word *wait* used in this verse is the same word as used in the phrase "waiting on tables" and "serving." Servants get tired. "They that wait upon the LORD shall renew their strength...they shall run, and not be weary; and they shall walk, and not faint" (Isa. 40:31). As you take the attitude of a servant in your work for the Lord, He will renew your strength.

Paul wrote to the Corinthians: "Our sufficiency is of God" (2 Cor. 3:5). A servant is always dependent on his master, never self-sufficient. We will soon run out of strength if we try to be sufficient in ourselves. God must become our sufficiency as we learn to depend on Him. The Greek word for *sufficiency* means "a warehouse with no back wall to it." When we get inside that warehouse, we start shouting about the "unsearchable riches of Christ...the breadth, and length, and depth, and height" (Eph. 3:8, 18) as Paul did. We can never exhaust God's sufficiency. However, we won't have a key to the warehouse without first having a servant spirit. As servants we are colaborers with God, and He becomes our sufficiency for service.

A SERVANT'S HEART

A servant is not someone who does something with gritted teeth or leaves skid marks along the way in following Jesus. He is not someone who does a certain task because he is not qualified to do something greater. Nor is he a person "put down" to a low status because of race, creed or color. A servant is someone who has *chosen* to reflect in his life the family image of God.

In the life of Abigail, we see a woman who displayed this family spirit. She had a very mean husband, a man who was a drunkard. (See 1 Samuel 25:3–10.) God judged him worthy of death for insulting David. As a result of her godly behavior, this precious wife received a message from King David after the death of her husband; he wanted her to become his wife. David was the king, the prophet, the priest, the sweet singer of Israel. He honored Abigail by asking her to become his wife. If we had received such an invitation, we might have published it in the newspaper, called reporters and dress designers and celebrated with parties. What an honor! When Abigail received the invitation, she bowed her face to the earth and showed her humility and submission, saying, "Behold, let thine handmaid be a servant" (1 Sam. 25:41). She was invited to become David's wife, yet her response to him was, "Let me be a servant to wash the feet of the servants of my lord." She could have immediately taken on an air of superiority, but instead she chose to respond in a spirit of humility.

Servanthood is determined by who you *are*, not by what you *do*. True servanthood involves heart reality. You must learn to see yourself and every other believer in relationship to the Lord Jesus Christ, rather than evaluating each other's worth by position or title. Every person must be valued for who he is, rather than for what he does. What you do is a result of who you are. That understanding may be contrary to your idea of who a servant is. Often we consider a hireling, someone who does hourly work and performs a task we would rather not perform, to be a servant. If we call people servants because of what they do, our idea of a servant must change. Servanthood is determined by who we are.

When you begin to see yourself primarily as a servant, it won't make any difference what you are asked to do. If you are to reflect the character of Jesus, you must develop a servant's heart. Can you humble yourself as Jesus did? He emptied Himself in eternity, stripping Himself of all privilege and every title, humbling Himself by choice to become the obedient Servant to carry out His Father's wishes. Because He was willing to humble Himself, the Father has highly honored Him. (See Philippians 2:7–9.)

Your place of authority with God, not just hereafter, but here on earth, will be determined by your having the attitude of a servant. When you know who God is, you will choose to serve Him above everything else on earth. One of the most beautiful examples of a servant spirit I have ever seen is in the life of the pastor with whom I left my church in Texas. The outstanding characteristic that my husband and I saw in Dr. Sam Sasser during the seven years before we asked him to come and pastor our church was his attitude of a servant. He never sought to be honored or seen as special. Though he is highly educated, having earned four doctorate degrees, in honor he always prefers others before himself. He has a servant spirit, and God has honored him by allowing him to minister in places where very few may go.

Our servant heart will be expressed in all our relationships. I love my husband, LeRoy Pickett. When he traveled with me, everywhere we went people would say to him, "This is 'Honey,' isn't it? We know you already." Pastors said to him, "That woman loves the ground you walk on." Do you think it is a chore for me to do something for him? A servant who is not a hireling doesn't always have to be told everything he has to do. He knows his master well enough to know what he wants and to do it.

Some of us have secretaries who are true servants. For several years, I had a secretary who anticipated what I would need before I ever got to the task. She was not waiting for me to come and tell her what to do. Very often she said to me, "I count it a privilege; I feel I have been honored to work with you." It was an honor to me to have her work for me. I took good care of her, because I knew I might never get another secretary like Judy. She was special. Servants are special. They are not hirelings or wage earners, but people who reflect the family spirit of God in their work and relationships.

THE GREATEST SERVANT

Becoming a servant means that by your choice you are "in honor preferring one another" (Rom. 12:10). Jesus preferred us above Himself, willingly suffering the supreme sacrifice of giving His life to redeem us. Paul admonished us to:

> Let this mind be in you, which was also in Christ Jesus: Who, being in the form of God, thought it not robbery to be equal with God: but made himself of no reputation, and took upon him the form of a servant.
>
> —PHILIPPIANS 2:5–7

In the garden of Gethsemane, Jesus revealed His servant heart when He prayed, "O my Father, if it be possible, let this cup pass from me: nevertheless not as I will, but as thou wilt" (Matt. 26:39). He did not pray this out of fear, as some teach. It is blasphemous to think there was cowardice in our Lord. Jesus knew He was the Lamb, "slain from the foundation of the world" (Rev. 13:8). He knew who He was and that He came to die. He went to the garden as the Servant and the Lamb.

Then why did He pray in that way? Is it possible that in that garden the Father revealed to Jesus that He would not only be the Lamb of God, but the Scapegoat as well? Once a year on the Day of Atonement the

Israelites took ashes of the sin offering and put them on the head of the scapegoat. They would then send that goat outside the city wall, never to be retrieved. This they did to atone, in type, for the sin principle in man that causes him to transgress. That night in the garden, did God unveil to Jesus that not only would He fulfill the sacrifice of the Lamb, to take away the sins of the world, but that of the Scapegoat as well, to redeem man from the sin principle? Jesus knew that the scape-goat was never retrieved. Was He expressing in His agony that night, "Father, if there is no other way to save Your family, I will not only be the sacrificed Lamb, I will become the Scapegoat as well. If there is no other way, I will go, never to come back"? He proved His explicit trust in the Father's will when He cried from the cross, "Father, into thy hands I commend my spirit" (Luke 23:46).

Moses prayed, "Yet now, if thou wilt forgive their sin ... and if not, blot me, I pray thee, out of thy book which thou hast written" (Exod. 32:32). In the life of the ser-vant Moses, we see the willingness to have his own name blotted out in order for God's people to be res-cued. The apostle Paul declared that he could wish him-self accursed and cut off from Christ for the sake of his brothers (Rom. 9:3). It is impossible that mere human ministers would experience a more sacrificial love for mankind than their Lord. Our twofold redemption was fulfilled on Calvary, the sin principle destroyed. Paul declared to us in the Book of Romans: "For the law of the Spirit of life in Christ Jesus hath made me free from the law of sin and death" (Rom. 8:2).

Jesus became the greatest Servant of all by humbling

Himself to become man and the servant of men, and then giving His life as the perfect sacrifice for mankind's redemption. On the eve of His death, during the last supper with His disciples, He gave us one more glimpse of the family spirit. *Knowing* that the Father had given all things into His hands, Jesus took a towel and girded Himself and washed His disciples' feet (John 13:4–5). After His resurrection from the dead, having won the supreme victory over sin, Jesus still revealed the humble servant spirit to His disciples the morning He cooked their breakfast on the shore of the lake. The disciples had gone fishing. "As soon as they were come to land, they saw a fire of coals there, and fish laid thereon, and bread. Jesus saith unto them…Come and dine" (John 21:9–12). That servant spirit is the nature of the family of God. Jesus never manifested any other spirit.

We call servanthood an unpopular doctrine because to embrace it requires death to our selfish natures, our desire to rule. In order for you to be changed into the likeness of Jesus, you must become a servant. I didn't learn this truth in school. As seminary students, we dreamed of becoming great ministers or pastors. Our true call, however, is to be like Jesus, who chose to become a servant. The greatest role to which you can aspire is to be changed into the likeness of Jesus and become a servant. As you allow the Holy Spirit to work on your nature, you will reflect the character of Jesus in your life.

---

1. Sue Curran, *The Forgiving Church* (Blountville, TN: Shekinah Publishers, 1990), vii.

Chapter 5

THE CHARACTER
OF GOD'S PURPOSE

Responding to the call to servanthood involves scrutinizing the attitudes and motivations that form the basis of our character. Solomon taught that "as [a man] thinketh in his heart, so is he" (Prov. 23:7). If in our hearts we see ourselves as wonderful people with tremendous potential for becoming great in some sphere of life or ministry, we have not yet responded to the call to servanthood. When you see yourself as a blood-bought child of God, no longer belonging to yourself, your response will be, "Lord, I love You enough to serve You." A true servant heart pursues *holiness* and *purity of motive* in service.

Sometimes people serve with mixed motives. If you are doing a task to receive recognition for it, you are not doing it with a servant spirit. Paul wrote to the Ephesians, "Slaves, obey your earthly masters with respect and fear, and with sincerity of heart, just as you would obey Christ" (Eph. 6:5, NIV). God is looking for one who serves to please Christ. Some serve out of a desire to get "brownie points." My former staff used to tease each other about doing something special for "Pastor." They would say, "Aha, you are trying to get brownie points to earn her favor." We serve God because we love Him, not to earn His favor.

Others serve because they are attempting to "work out their own salvation." You need to understand that you don't serve to get to heaven. That is still difficult for me to grasp because of my religious background. I somehow feel that if I can serve Him better, I can merit His favor. However, that is not how we merit His favor. We must be cleansed of this kind of thinking. We must not attend church because of what the pastor will think of us if we don't. We should not give our tithes because someone will see the record and know how we gave. We give because we love the One who gave us life, even if no one sees the record.

Your motivation for serving is as important as your service, for God is looking for servant hearts to reflect the spirit of the Lamb. As you allow the Holy Spirit to teach you to become part of the family of God, He will change your motivation and your attitude to reflect the Lamb spirit. Paul taught us what the fruit of a Spirit-filled life would look like when he wrote, "But the fruit of the Spirit is love, joy, peace, longsuffering, gentleness, goodness, faith, meekness, temperance: against such there is no law" (Gal. 5:22–23).

A true servant will be motivated by love. I want to be able to sing in the same way an elderly, gray-headed professor sang who taught me in college. He would come into our Pentateuch class and, without any formality of opening remarks, would bow his head, shake his gray hair and sing, "He loves me, He loves me, He loves me this I know; He gave Himself to die for me, because He loves me so."[1] We students would end up

on the cement floor crying our eyes out because of the
presence of God that filled the classroom. When he got
through singing, we didn't think we knew God at all.
He was the most brilliant man of the college, and the
most humble. On workdays, he was present. When
there were leaves to be raked, he was there. They would
say, "Dr. Burkholder, you don't need to do that."

He would reply, "Oh, but I do. I am doing it for
Jesus." Everywhere he went he could be heard singing,
"He loves me, He loves me."

CHARACTERISTICS OF A SERVANT

If we serve the Lord selfishly for what He gives us, then
we would serve the devil just as willingly if he paid
higher wages. If our motivation for serving God is that
He blesses and heals and prospers us, we are display-
ing the spirit of the hireling. Those who respond to
the call to servanthood serve Jesus because they love
Him. When we love ourselves more than we love God,
we are not willing to become servants. Love slaves
have a supreme desire that the Master know they are
serving because they love Him.

Joy

Joy is the desired attitude of a servant. "The joy of the
LORD is your strength" (Neh. 8:10). According to Dr.
David Schoch, that verse literally reads, "The joy we
experience in serving God gives us back our strength."[2]
God's genuine approval of our service becomes strength
for us to serve. A servant does each task joyfully. He
doesn't stop working five minutes early, deciding not to
start something else because it is quitting time. Neither

is his attitude dependent upon his circumstances always being pleasant. It is written of Jesus, "Who for the joy that was set before him endured the cross" (Heb. 12:2). Jesus' suffering did not destroy His joy. A servant can endure great difficulty because he is convinced that his greatest privilege on earth is to serve God.

I loved my earthly daddy so much that it was a delight for me to serve him. I was delighted when he asked me, instead of my mother, to get his coffee. When he asked me to make him some cornbread, do you think I felt it was belittling? I practiced and practiced, dumping out one pan of cornbread after another until I could be sure I had made some that would please my daddy. It was my joy to serve him. If I could experience that joy in serving my earthly daddy, how much more should I rejoice in serving my heavenly Father? I am a daughter of God, and it is a supreme joy to serve Him. When we live as true servants, our service brings us pleasure; we don't complain over any menial task.

Faithfulness

Faithfulness further characterizes the servant heart. A servant is a faithful steward or overseer. A steward takes care of something that belongs to another person until that one can return to take care of it. As an overseer, he does not require the master to write out all the instructions, but is able to take on responsibility within a certain latitude. A servant develops as he works in an area, exploring its needs and responding to them. Every Christian has been given stewardship of a treasure within, that is, of the life of Jesus that God has invested in us. We are responsible to allow the character of Christ to be developed in us as we yield to the

Holy Spirit's conviction and prompting, showing us where we need to be changed. We will not be rewarded for our educational degrees or our personal excellence, but for our faithful obedience as servants.

Our greatest commendation will be for God to say to us, "Well done, thou good and faithful servant" (Matt. 25:21). He does not commend the preacher, apostle or minister—He commends the *servant*. Whether or not we have succeeded in man's eyes, if we earn *God's commendation* we have truly succeeded in life.

I knew a man who gave a beautiful piano concert one evening. When he had finished, everyone in the auditorium stood to give an ovation except for one man. The musician left the auditorium sadly with his head down. Someone later remarked to him about the wonderful ovation he had received. He replied that he didn't think it was wonderful. The friend reminded him that everyone in the auditorium had stood to congratulate him. The musician answered, "There was one who did not stand, and he was my *teacher*. I would rather he had stood than all the others." There is only One whose commendation the true servant of God wants to hear, and that is God's. If all the other people think we are wonderful, but we have not pleased our Father, we will have failed.

On the day I stand before the Master, I want to hear Him say, "Well done, good and faithful servant." I began praying to hear Him say that many years ago when He called me and said, "If you love Me, feed My sheep."

We respond to the servant call by being willing to feed His sheep. However, sheep aren't always very nice. There are a lot of things we could do that would seem more worthwhile than feeding sheep. One night when I was praying and telling the Lord how much I loved Him, He said to me, "I know you love Me; you are feeding My sheep." Our measure of love is not found in how many gifts we have or how highly someone thinks of us. We evaluate our love by our faithfulness to obey what He has asked us to do.

Faithfulness results in our becoming addicted to service. In the New Testament we read of the house of Stephanas, where each family member had addicted himself or herself to ministry. The Greek reads, "They made up their minds to serve as servants; they were addicted." (See 1 Corinthians 16:15.) When you are addicted to something, you feel as though you can't live without it. The house of Stephanas could not live without serving; they were addicted to it.

Humility

If joy is our attitude, and faithfulness our measure of love, we can describe *humility* as the demeanor of our servant heart. A proud spirit will rarely be joyful, nor will it be faithful to any task that does not satisfy its ego. A love slave is willing to keep a low profile without needing a title for everything he does. He produces what the Father wants without exalting himself by using titles. I dislike the way some people refer to themselves as *apostles* or *prophets*. Although it is true that Paul referred to himself as an apostle, he also called himself *a servant to the Lord*. I would rather just *do* the ministry and let someone else decide what to call it. The spirit of our Father's family is not a spirit of exaltation or pride, but this spirit is exemplified in the spirit of the Lamb who sacrificed Himself to redeem us. Humility characterizes those who are full of the Holy Spirit. The spirit of the family of God is the spirit of the prodigal son who has come to himself, is broken and is anxious to come home to his daddy, saying, "Make me as one of thy hired servants" (Luke 15:19).

When I was practicing nursing in Eden, North Carolina, a precious man whom I had known from my childhood was admitted to the hospital as a patient. He was Dr. William Gordon, an Episcopal priest in our city. It would take a lot of space to tell you the things this man did in our little town that proved to everyone he was a man of God. I don't know anyone else who ever graced our city with the Spirit of Christ like this man did. He wore his vestments on Sunday; he stood in his pomp and said his prayers from his prayer book. But Monday night at midnight, when no one was looking, he would be down in the poor section of town, where he could be seen picking up a coal scuttle to take someone some coal. The cobbler told me that many times Dr. Gordon would walk into his business with a little boy from the poor section of town and say, "Would you half-sole his shoes?" Often the cobbler looked at the priest's shoes and saw that there were larger holes in them than in the boy's.

When this priest became a patient in the hospital, the staff respected him so much they assigned the superintendent of nurses to give him his bath. She told me that as she bathed his feet, tears dripped down her cheeks because of the regard she had for him. When he died, stores closed, businesses sent flowers, and government offices in Raleigh closed for the day to honor him. A servant of God had made his mark on our city.

May God help us to leave the mark of one who picks up the towel and washes the feet of others. Humility is a beautiful attribute of the servant heart. Without humility there is no true servanthood. God is calling for servants who will be filled with the fruit of the Holy Spirit. He is not seeking those who desire honor and recognition, but those who serve Him because they love Him supremely.

A Servant's Garment

You cannot respond to the call to servanthood without being secure in your identity as a person. Without knowing who you are in God, you will never choose to become a servant. That is why the understanding of God's eternal purpose for you is so important. It gives meaning and purpose to your life and sets you free to become a servant of God. The greater the understanding you have of who you are, the less you feel you have to "prove" to yourself and others.

The Scripture says that on the night of the last supper with His disciples:

> Jesus *knowing* that the Father had given all things into his hands, and that he was come from God, and went to God; he riseth from supper, and laid aside his garments; and took a towel, and girded himself. After that he poureth water into a basin, and began to wash the disciples' feet, and to wipe them with the towel wherewith he was girded.
>
> —JOHN 13:3–5, EMPHASIS ADDED

Jesus knew who He was and that everything in the world belonged to Him. With that knowledge, He rose from supper, took a towel, poured water into a basin and began to wash the disciples' feet.

When we know who we are, we can do as Jesus did. A strong sense of identity and a healthy self-esteem make us willing to humble ourselves to become servants. Because of self-conceit and pride, some Christians render themselves useless in the kingdom. Great churches and big ministries have fallen when leaders became exalted through pride. Only by humbling yourself to become a servant can you avoid falling to pride. The apostle Paul warned, "For I say, through the grace given unto me, to every man that is among you, not to think of himself more highly than he ought to think" (Rom. 12:3).

It is important to realize that a servant's garment is fitted to size, tailor-made by God for each servant. No one else can wear yours. Once you get that robe on, it has the sweetest aroma of any garment you can wear, because servants go to the garden to pick spices for the king. (See Song of Solomon 1:12.) We must also understand that the garment of a servant is not to be worn on certain occasions only, or in special situations. Some people will serve the pastor or officials in the church, but they won't willingly serve someone else for fear of not receiving any recognition for what they do. As we have seen, recognition is not the goal of the servant heart.

Another fact about the servant's garment is that we don't have to worry about putting it under lock and key. A servant's robe is never stolen. Though people may stand in line to get your position, they will not do so to get your servant's robe. There are enough servants' garments for all who will humble themselves to respond to the call to servanthood. Servants don't have to make good impressions; they are known by the garments they wear.

A servant's garment carries with it a lovely aroma. There is nothing more fragrant than a *poured-out life*. Helen Vincent Washburn lived such a life. I was privileged to sit at her feet for four years. Besides being the greatest teacher I have ever heard, she was the most beautiful woman I have ever seen, with clear blue eyes, blond hair and fair complexion. She was the epitome of charm and grace and could mingle with the most highly cultured or the least cultured of this country without embarrassing anyone. The poor man would be as totally comfortable with her as would more prominent people.

Her teaching ministry made me hungry for the Word. The truths she taught me were the same truths the Holy Spirit brought back to my remembrance after I received the baptism of the Holy Spirit. But what impressed me more than anything else was that she was a servant. I have seen her wash peoples' clothes and do things other people would not do. She wasn't too good to clean, sweep, cook or do whatever needed to be done. Her philosophy, which I hope she instilled in me, and that I have tried to instill in the students in our Bible school, was, "Whatsoever your hands find to do, do it." She wore her servant's garment well and blessed many with her poured-out life.

THE WOMB OF SERVICE—WORSHIP

Our response to the call to servanthood also depends on our becoming true worshipers of God, for our service is born out of the womb of worship. It is not possible to be rightly motivated, or to have the attitude of a servant, without first being birthed into a relationship of worship to the living God. The Scriptures declare, "Thou shalt worship the Lord thy God, and him only shalt thou serve" (Luke 4:8). That commandment teaches us that worshiping God and serving Him are closely related. We can see the cross in this command. Worshiping the Lord shows our vertical relationship to God, while the horizontal command, "him only shalt thou serve," stretches us to reach out to mankind. He further taught us that, "Inasmuch as ye have done it unto one of the least of these my brethren, ye have done it unto me" (Matt. 25:40). Your witness and your worship are determined by your servanthood. *You will worship God no higher than you know Him. You will know Him no higher than you serve Him.* As you worship God, your love for Him will grow, and you will desire to find ways to serve Him in order to express that love.

Scripture gives us fourteen ways to express worship with our physical body. However, learning how to express yourself to God in fourteen different ways is not necessarily worship. Worship is a way of life, the result of serving. The highest worship is the given life of a servant. Paul declared, "I beseech you therefore, brethren, by the mercies of God, that you present your bodies a living sacrifice, holy, acceptable unto God, which is your reasonable service" (Rom. 12:1). He is not speaking merely of coming to church to give a sacrifice of the fruit of your lips in praising God. Your very life must become a sacrifice. If your life is a living sacrifice, worship will be a spontaneous overflow of who you are.

Service is an evidence of the way you worship. When you serve the body of Christ, you show that you love God. There is no way you can love Him and not serve your fellowman, as well as your brothers and sisters in the church. My Father has shown me that when I stand before Him, the rewards I receive for every service I have conducted and every life I have touched will be shared by Fountain Gate Ministries, Shekinah Ministries and others who have become a part of my service for God. These ministries had a part in sending me out, and they pray for me. We are servants together. If we serve with singleness of motive, doing the will of God with our whole soul, our reward will be as great as the reward for those who we think have done something greater than we have done. If we serve a prophet, we share the prophet's reward. (See Matthew 10:41.) True worship is costly; it will cost your life being poured out as a servant to do anything for Jesus, night or day, that He asks you to do.

GOD IDENTIFIES HIS LEADERS AS SERVANTS

Your thinking will be transformed from the worldly pursuit of greatness when you understand. God often refers to great men as *His servants*. Although many great things were written about David, in the New Testament he is called, "His [God's] servant David" (Luke 1:69, NKJV). Moses, the great deliverer of Israel, is spoken of as, "Moses the servant" (Josh. 1:1). God was not demeaning the worth of this mighty deliverer, as we might think, but commending him in his relationship to God. Becoming a servant of God had required great transformation of Moses' character. He had to be

changed before he received God's commendation as
the meekest man on earth. Joshua, Moses' successor, is
called *Moses' servant.* We may assume that he learned
much about leadership from Moses.

The prophet Elisha served under Elijah faithfully
before receiving his request for a double portion of
Elijah's spirit. We read that Elisha "poured water on the
hands of Elijah" (2 Kings 3:11). What a lowly job, keep-
ing the hands of the prophet clean. But the hour came
when the old prophet asked his young servant what he
could do for him. Elisha asked for a double portion of
Elijah's spirit and received it from God. (See 2 Kings
2:9.) Servants receive mantles and double portions.

The apostle Paul, in expressing his service to the
church at Ephesus, bowed himself in humility and
said that with many tears and temptations he *served*
his people (Acts 20:19). If it can be said of me when I
leave this world, "She was a woman full of the Spirit
of the Lord who served God without guile," that
would be the greatest compliment anyone could give
me. I would rather people did not speak of what I did,
but of who I was, a woman with the family spirit, a
faithful servant.

Jesus became the Servant in eternity before He
came to earth. His very nature is that of a servant.
That which He did in eternity was reflected in the
washing of His disciples' feet during His last supper
with them. Are you willing to allow the servant attitude expressed by Jesus to be yours? Are you willing to
"stoop" to that which is a reversal of the world's
system? The world doesn't wash feet. Will you choose
to have the family spirit? After Jesus chose to take the

seven steps downward, God exalted Him and gave Him "a name which is above every name" (Phil. 2:9). Everyone who humbles himself shall be exalted.

I feel I am highly honored to have the privilege of sharing with so many of my Father's family and to meet so many precious brothers and sisters, as well as God's chosen ministers. I never dreamed I would go where I have been able to go or that God would give me the honor to serve where I have had the privilege of serving. I have the honor of bearing my Master's name, and I want to be known as His servant. The greatest thing we can aspire to on earth is to be classified by God as *His servant.* Then we'll hear Him say, "Henceforth I call you not servants…I have called you friends" (John 15:15). The love slave with the bored ear will hear what is in the Father's heart and be a part of fulfilling God's purpose, for God talks to His friends.

KNOWING THE MASTER

A servant can best represent his master if he knows him well. When he stays close to the master, a servant understands all his master's moods and knows what he likes and doesn't like. He knows the master better than anyone else.

One precious girl who worked for me is as dear to me as any sister on earth. Gracie worked for me for six years when I pastored in North Carolina. She had another job from 3 P.M. to 11 P.M. each night. But she became my friend and said, "My pastor needs me." Every morning by 8 A.M. she would arrive at my home. Until 1 P.M. every day, she took care of my child, my household, all the guests and me. At that time I had not yet been healed from an illness that threatened my life, and I spent much of my time in the hospital. Many times Gracie came by the house late at night or in the wee hours of the morning, picked me up, bathed me and held me when I fainted. She had a true servant heart and was a trusted friend.

Years later when my first husband went to heaven, she came to my home and asked my son, "Is your mommy here?"

My son said, "Yes, and she is going to be delighted to see you." He told me that Gracie was there to see me and brought her right in.

I said, "Gracie, wasn't my husband a wonderful man?"

She looked at me and said, "Nobody knows like you and I know."

Who is going to represent our Master—hirelings or "big shots"? There is a spirit in every one of us that wants to rule. If you don't believe it, get into a car with six people to go eat lunch and see who decides where to go. There is a spirit in man that wants to rule woman, because that is the fallen nature. If we women can't get our way "legitimately," we will try pouting. We all want to be "in charge." Christians should have a totally different spirit from the spirit that wants to rule. The spirit of the family is a servant spirit. If we are going to be like our Father when we get home, we will have to let the Holy Spirit develop in us the spirit of the servant. Another way of describing it is a *lamb spirit.*

The spirit of the household is not one of *independence.* God told me that He had kicked the spirit of independence out of heaven, and He won't let it back in. We say that the first sin is pride, but it is not. Pride is a result of independence and wanting to rule. All sin comes out of the desire to rule and to be worshiped.

No wonder God wants us to become servants. Servanthood will solve the sin question. Having a servant spirit will destroy the sin principle at work in us. You won't have a servant spirit unless you take your self life to the cross and there exchange your self life for the Christ life. Do you really want to have the Spirit of Christ? The Spirit of Christ is the spirit of a servant who, by choice, humbled Himself. Someone once said that Jesus prayed for God to make Him humble. God doesn't do that. He tells us to humble *ourselves*, and He will exalt us. (See James 4:10.) A servant is someone who stoops low enough to be great enough to receive the family spirit.

Your home will be transformed into a refuge of peace and comfort when you lay down your desire to rule and humble yourself to respond to the call to servanthood. Then you will begin to know God's purpose for the home and family, and to walk in His divine order for mankind, which will make your days as days of heaven on earth.

---

1. "He Loves Me" by Isaac Watts. Public Domain.
2. *Matthew Henry's Commentary on the Whole Bible,* New Modern Edition, Electronic Database (Hendrickson Publishers, Inc., 1991).

Chapter 6

PURPOSE UNENCUMBERED
BY TRADITION

I t deeply concerns me that people often study their
Bibles through eyes of prejudice, custom and tradition. They read into the Scriptures what they have been
taught, instead of *coming in faith* with an open heart
and mind to hear what the Holy Spirit meant. The
apostle Paul declared, "Before faith came, we were kept
under the law, shut up unto the faith which should
afterwards be revealed" (Gal. 3:23). People can't understand the Word until faith has been revealed to them
because tradition, prejudice, culture, denominationalism, pseudo-masculinism and other bondages of the
carnal mind hinder them. After faith comes, we are no
longer under the law, but we walk in the grace Jesus
brought to us through redemption.

Paul told the Galatians, "But after faith is come, we
are no longer under a schoolmaster. For ye are all the
children of God by faith in Christ Jesus" (Gal.
3:25–26). Then he added, "There is neither Jew nor
Greek…there is neither male nor female: for ye are all
one in Christ Jesus" (Gal. 3:28).

Faith comprehends God's intentions in creating
mankind. The Fall of man has so damaged us that we

are quite unaware of the purpose for which God created man. We are oblivious to the divine order that He intended for man and woman to enjoy. Until faith comes to our hearts we cannot expect an illumination of the Word of God that gives us understanding of the purposes of God. The Scriptures teach that "the natural man receiveth not the things of the Spirit of God: for they are foolishness unto him: neither can he know them, because they are spiritually discerned" (1 Cor. 2:14). We should not wonder, then, that the church, which has not yet come into a proper relationship with the Holy Spirit, is living without true understanding of God's divine order for mankind.

God's Divine Order for *Mankind*

A basic misunderstanding arises from our definition of *man*. In the Hebrew, the word *man* has no gender to it, but is translated as our word *mankind*. "And the Lord God said, It is not good that the man should be alone; I will make him an help meet for him" (Gen. 2:18). Now God is going to do surgery to separate mankind into two sexes. In mankind was "male" and "female." You cannot understand male and female if you don't understand "mankind." When God made a help meet for Adam, He caused a deep sleep to fall upon him. Then He took one of Adam's ribs, and from that rib made a woman and brought her unto the man. Adam said, "This is now bone of my bones, and flesh of my flesh: she shall be called Woman, because she was taken out of Man" (v. 23). The next verse teaches that God's purpose was for them to be one. God brought the woman *unto* the man, not *under* him. She was to walk beside him and be one with him. God ordained that woman should be a "help meet" for the man. One of the Hebrew words for *help meet* is *reflection*. That is a beautiful picture of God's divine intention in creating mankind to walk together as one in fellowship with God.

The woman was not named Eve until after they fell by disobedience to God's command. God did not name the woman. Adam named her Eve after the Fall, so the fallen woman is Eve. As God's plan for redemption unfolds, we realize that to be a part of the bride of Christ, we must be redeemed from that fallen "Eve" nature. Christ is going to take a wife, but she is not going to be "Eve." We are born again in Christ, who is called the "last Adam," to become one with Him, redeemed from the curse that came upon mankind because of disobedience.

The serpent beguiled the woman in the garden, and she and her husband partook of the forbidden tree. After that, "they heard the voice of the LORD God walking in the garden in the cool of the day: and Adam and his wife hid themselves from the presence of the LORD God amongst the trees of the garden" (Gen. 3:8). Both the man and the woman heard God coming and hid from Him.

It is interesting that in our tradition and prejudice we say that the woman cannot hear God, that man must hear Him and tell the woman what He said. Yet the Scriptures do not teach that as God's divine order for mankind. Adam *and his wife* fellowshiped together with the voice of God in the garden until the time of their disobedience. We do not know how long they lived before falling to sin, but God visited them until then.

Both genders of mankind were confronted by God and received separate judgments because of the wrong-doing. Adam "pointed the finger" at his wife when God confronted him, declaring, "The woman whom thou gavest to be with me, she gave me of the tree, and I did eat" (Gen. 3:12). Here began the tragic controversy between the sexes, which has raged mercilessly through-out the history of man. It has run from the extremes of so demeaning women in some cultures that they are of less value than animals, to demanding in other cul-tures that they be given the status of men in every way, thereby threatening the very basis of womanhood. There is little peace or harmony in the best of situations between male and female, much less the "oneness" that God declared as His intention for mankind. Even in the church, where redemption is working, we still come short of Paul's declaration that in Christ there is neither male nor female. We continue to speak to "issues" regarding the acceptable role of women in the ministry of the church, demonstrating that we have not "come to faith." We have accepted the plight of fallen man as God's divine order for the church.

When God confronted the woman because of her disobedience, He indicated several ways she would suffer as a fallen woman. In speaking to the serpent, He said, "And I will put enmity between thee and the woman, and between thy seed and her seed; it shall bruise thy head, and thou shalt bruise his heel" (Gen. 3:15). I believe the devil hates women more than men. God didn't say He would put enmity between the serpent and the man. The enmity is between the serpent and the woman, because the woman's seed would eventually crush the devil. Even in this judgment for sin, however, a loving God is speaking His promise of redemption. He determined to use a virgin to bear the Son that would bruise Satan's head. Then the devil hated the woman because she was going to bring forth the Son, and now he hates the church, because she is going to bring forth the Son again. As we have mentioned, especially where Christianity is not part of a culture, women have suffered terrible abuse through the centuries under the influence of satanically inspired cultures. Every time a woman gives birth to a baby, God's family has the possibility of being enlarged. (We should not wonder who is influencing the zero birth rate trends of many nations, convincing couples not to have children.)

God continued addressing the fallen woman, saying, "I will greatly multiply thy sorrow and thy conception; in sorrow thou shalt bring forth children; and thy desire shall be to thy husband, and he shall rule over thee" (Gen. 3:16). God was not revealing His divine order for the woman, but imposing on her the consequences of her fall. He was telling us how a *fallen* man and woman were going to relate to each other.

Restored to His Image

The fallen man would rule the woman, and she would desire him. In today's culture we see the fallen woman chasing the man more blatantly than ever. The natural woman feels she has to have a man, not to be a help meet to him as was purposed in the beginning, but to tempt and allure him through her passion and lust with the goal of controlling him. And the natural man's desire is to conquer the woman, to rule over her. That is all part of fallen life. So the woman must prepare to live under the fallen man, because as long as he is fallen, he will seek to rule over her. It is amazing that even in the church we have accepted as divine order for the home the premise that men are to rule their households. That is not in the Book, but is the desire of the fallen nature. Results of the Fall of man can never be construed as God's divine order for him. God told Adam he was going to eat by the sweat of his brow, but that was a consequence of sin rather than God's divine intention for him. God had purposed that mankind eat of the vegetation in the beautiful garden He had prepared for them and have dominion over every living thing.

In the garden, man was neither moral nor immoral, but was created amoral. He was given the power of choice, because God wanted us to choose to love Him freely, not out of compulsion. Mankind failed the love test when the first pair disobeyed the command of God not to eat of the tree of the knowledge of good and evil. Through their wrong choice, mankind became immoral. But God's eternal purpose was not thwarted, for He had anticipated Adam's failure before the foundation of the world and had prepared a Savior for mankind.

John assures us: "For this purpose the Son of God was manifested, that he might destroy the works of the devil" (1 John 3:8). That word *destroy* is the Greek word *louso*, which means, "to loose, to undo, outdo and overdo"—so are we to destroy everything the devil has ever done. When we accept Christ as our Savior, we are restored to the image of God. Restoration is a wonderful reality that promises that we will become all that God ordained for us to become in His eternal purpose.

My son, Darrell, has a hobby of restoring old cars. When they are completely restored, they are perfect representations of what the designers intended them to be, no matter how decrepit they were when the work of restoration began. If we can believe that God is perfectly restoring us to His image to reflect His will, we can rejoice even in our trials. We will experience what mankind would have known if the first pair had walked on with God and not fallen.

There was nothing to which Jesus laid the ax more violently than the traditions of men. Because of bondage to tradition, some cannot understand that there is no difference between male and female, for they have not come to faith. Paul declared that when we come to faith we will understand that there is neither Greek nor barbarian, male nor female, but we are all one in Christ Jesus. God is preparing men and women alike to be filled with His Spirit in the fullness of time, and He is delivering us from tradition, prejudice, culture and denominationalism.

We have tried to lay a guilt trip on men by telling them they are to fulfill every desire and deepest need of a woman. Men have been put into bondage by the expectation of their wives to meet every need of their lives. Though husbands should meet the physical and emotional needs of their wives, they cannot be expected to meet their spiritual needs. That is not God's divine order. Both man and woman are to walk together as one and let God fulfill the cry of their spirits for a true Bridegroom.

Many men have been gloriously delivered from the burden that some marriage counselors put upon them to meet their wife's every need. That was not God's intention. God ordained that man and woman should walk with Him and be as one, and He would meet the innermost needs of both of them. Divine order is higher than the plight of fallen man. It is far more liberating to men and women than having to live under the doctrine of the curse of a fallen Adam and a fallen Eve.

We have been redeemed to be one flesh in Him, bought with a price so that husbands and wives can truly become one. Paul admonishes us:

> Submitting yourselves one to another in the fear of God. Wives, submit yourselves unto your own husbands, as unto the Lord. For the husband is the head of the wife, even as Christ is the head of the church: and he is the saviour of the body. Therefore as the church is subject unto Christ, so let the wives be to their own husbands in every thing.
>
> —EPHESIANS 5:21–24

God said the husband is the head of the wife. We have called him the priest of the home, but the Bible does not teach that. The Bible teaches we are all part of a royal priesthood, to "shew forth the praises of him who hath called you out of darkness into his marvelous light" (1 Pet. 2:9). To say the husband is the "head" and not the "priest" is not a matter of semantics; it is a matter of assignment, of delegated authority.

I tell the men that they don't want me to preach about their delegated authority, because being the head of the home involves much more than being a priest. That wonderful realm of authority that God delegated is marvelous. But we must not give the man authority God didn't give him, or take away the authority that God did give him. God did not mean to put one gender of mankind over another, but for them to walk together as one, submitting themselves one to another.

This understanding does not destroy the order of the home; it does not touch delegated authority; it does not make women higher than men, or make them aggressive or domineering. It puts man and woman back together in Jesus. We do not need "Women's Lib" or ERA. They are only swapping places to rule instead of fallen man, who was not supposed to be ruling anyway. I want to be redeemed to God's purpose for mankind to become who I was made to be in God and walk beside the man with whom I am supposed to walk. In Christ, now, there is neither male nor female, but mankind, walking together.

After the Fall of man, when Adam named his wife Eve, we read, "This is the book of the generations of Adam...and Adam lived an hundred and thirty years, and begat a son in his own likeness, *after his image*" (Gen. 5:1, 3, emphasis added). Here we see the generations of Adam, not Jesus. He begat sons in his own image. We were born in the nature of Adam. The carnal nature comes from our father, Adam, not from our Father God. God knew we couldn't change ourselves back into His image, so He designed the costly plan of redemption through the blood of His own Son, Jesus. I spent seventeen years trying to act like Him. Two-thirds of the church world today is trying to "act" like Jesus.

We don't have that ability. Jesus was the express image of the Father, sent to live in us by the power of the Holy Spirit until that image takes over our inner natures—our spirits and souls. He begins to change us from glory to glory. When He fills our beings, as He wanted to do before man ever fell, we are going to go home in His image, complete and mature.

The more I am willing to give up my image, the more of God's image I can receive. "Good-bye, Adam. Today I'm not going to have your image. I do not vote for you; you are dead, and dead people do not talk. Today the image of God is going to be allowed to operate in my life." Being changed from glory to glory is not the same as being challenged. Being challenged won't take you home in His image; only change will do that. By the action of Calvary, we are being changed into Christ's image so male and female can walk together as one, each with his or her own delegated authority.

God puts both of them back into Christ, not as male and female, but as mankind, walking with God. Husband and wife, male and female preacher, man and woman leader will walk in the cool of the day with Jesus who is talking to us, fellowshiping with us, giving us authority and changing us into His image. In the last Adam, God is restoring what we would have had if Adam had not fallen in the beginning. It is glorious indeed to see God restoring men and women together as "one," seeing them fulfill their delegated responsibilities, yet both being the servants that He has called them to be.

As God delivers His church from the bondages of

tradition and culture and from fallen man's doctrine of divine order, we will see men and women function together to build godly homes and to fulfill God's purpose for the building of His church. As redemption cleanses us from the desire to rule, man and woman will not be threatened by each other, but will welcome the godly counsel of one another.

The Bible gives many examples of women who provided godly leadership. Deborah was set by God as a judge, a prophetess and a general in the army. She was able to tell Barak what God had said to her, and Barak then declared he would not go to battle without her. (See Judges 4:4–8.) Deborah was a woman who knew where to be and when to be, and who stayed with God until the right time came. I believe in these last days of God's outpouring of His Spirit, many Baraks will say to their Deborahs that they will not go to battle without them. I feel it is the timing of God to restore man and woman back to the divine order in the home and in the kingdom of God. I believe they will walk together as one under God's mandate, to tend the garden, multiply, take dominion over every living thing, and, as the bride of Christ, prepare for His coming. It is the hour for man and woman to come to faith, to stop living under fallen doctrine and to start living according to divine order.

Over the past few years I have begun to see some interesting changes in the church. More men and women are working together as copastors than I have seen in all my previous years of ministry. Men who are being restored are realizing there are two of us, and no one is usurping the other's delegated authority. God pours out His Spirit on His sons and His daughters alike. We are in Christ, the last Adam who didn't fail, and in Him everything is being restored to fulfill God's dream.

Chapter 7

PURPOSE
REDEEMED

The truths that Jesus taught through parables are like stones thrown into a mirrored pond, creating ever-widening ripples on the water. The physical elements of the parables are like the stones, and the truths they teach like the ripples on the water. The Holy Spirit has come to lead us into all truth. As you cultivate your relationship with Him, He opens the Scriptures to give greater understanding than you have previously grasped.

Sometimes we see only the *stones* of truth and do not comprehend the larger meaning reflected in the *ripples*. For example, in the parable of the lost sheep, the lost coin and the lost son, many of His hearers saw only the physical elements of the story. (See Luke 15.) They understood that the shepherd was concerned enough for his lost sheep that he left the others to go and find it, and they rejoiced with the woman who lost her coin and swept until she found it. They empathized with the father whose son had left and was now returning. But they did not see beyond the literal characters of the story to the truth Jesus was teaching.

Others have seen the first few ripples on the water

and applied their understanding to the significance of the lost sheep representing a lost sinner for whom the chief Shepherd searches until He brings him safely home. Likewise, with the lost coin and the lost son, we have applied this truth to lost sinners finding their way home to God. This is certainly a valid understanding, for Jesus came to "seek and to save that which was lost" (Luke 19:10). However, the Holy Spirit is enlarging our understanding of truth and giving us prophetic insight into what Jesus was teaching that applies specifically to the church today.

GOD'S PURPOSE FOR HIS CHURCH

The stories of the lost sheep, the lost coin and the lost son actually comprise one parable. When Jesus' presence drew a crowd, the Scripture says He spoke *this* parable to them. Although the parable includes three different subjects, in order to fully understand His intent, we must relate them to a single truth that Jesus was teaching. The complete significance of His teaching will be captured only as we grasp the composite picture He painted in the entire parable. As the Holy Spirit opens our understanding, we lose sight of the physical elements of these picture stories and begin to see clearly a larger truth regarding the fulfillment of God's purpose for His church. Jesus never lost sight of the ultimate purpose for which He had come, and every word He spoke related to the fulfilling of that purpose.

The lost sheep

In this parable, Jesus gave a beautiful prophetic word concerning what will happen in the church age.

He began by describing a shepherd who has lost a
sheep:

> What man of you, having an hundred sheep, if he
> lose one of them, doth not leave the ninety and
> nine in the wilderness, and go after that which is
> lost, until he find it? And when he hath found it,
> he layeth it on his shoulders, rejoicing. And when
> he cometh home, he calleth together his friends
> and neighbours, saying unto them, Rejoice with
> me; for I have found my sheep which was lost. I
> say unto you, that likewise joy shall be in heaven
> over one sinner that repenteth, more than over
> ninety and nine just persons, which need no
> repentance.
>
> —LUKE 15:4–7

Jesus refers to Himself as the good Shepherd who
lays down His life for His sheep. The Scriptures often
refer to Christ's followers as sheep. Peter exhorts elders
of the church to feed the "flock" of God, promising,
"When the chief Shepherd shall appear, ye shall receive
a crown of glory that fadeth not away" (1 Pet. 5:4). So
we may consider the church to be a sheepfold where
there is safety and care for each sheep, as well as food
and provision. Sheep require much care because they
are among the dumbest animals in the world, capable
of wandering away, losing their direction and getting
themselves into dangerous situations. They need the
care of a shepherd. Jesus is the chief Shepherd, and He
has given pastors to the church who have shepherds'
hearts. They will care for His sheep, feed them and pro-
tect them from wolves and other enemies.

God is bringing the church back to the leadership of

the chief Shepherd, under whom He places an under-shepherd. I am referring to a true shepherd who leads a local church, rather than a dominating ruler who dictates his will to people. There is a vast difference between dictatorship and true leadership. A true shepherd leads, feeds, protects and cares for the sheep. God places true shepherds where He wants them for as long as He needs them, and He moves them when His purposes are accomplished. He declares them to be gifts to the church, not to "freelancers" who say they don't need a church. God is intent on putting sheep under a shepherd because every sheep needs a sheepfold. The hour has come when we must be established in the local church, listen to the voice of the chief Shepherd and be led by undershepherds.

The shepherd in this parable put the lost sheep on his shoulders and carried her home. The original language gave the beautiful understanding that when the shepherd put the lost sheep on his shoulders, he carried her home safe and sound, fully restored. The shoulder, as generally used in Scripture, represents strength, succor, security, soundness, serenity and the sovereignty of government. The prophet Isaiah wrote of Jesus, "But he was wounded for our transgressions, he was bruised for our iniquities: the chastisement of our peace was upon him; and with his stripes we are healed. All we like sheep have gone astray…and the LORD hath laid on him the iniquity of us all" (Isa. 53:5–6). Jesus' back bore the pain of a cruel beating so that we could know healing.

I believe with all my heart that the days ahead are going to be days of great healing, for Jesus is not only going to heal people's bodies, but also their psyches and their homes. I am weary of people nursing and justifying their hurts. It doesn't matter if they inherited it from Grandma or Grandpa, how long they have had it, whether it was child abuse or a wound inflicted by the church or a preacher. I believe if we appropriate the provision of the wounded shoulder of the Shepherd, we can go home healed, safe and sound. It will be beautiful to see the Shepherd pick up His wandering sheep, the church, put her on His shoulder and arrive home, restored to all He has purposed for her.

The lost coin

Jesus continued His teaching:

> Either what woman having ten pieces of silver, if she lose one piece, doth not light a candle, and sweep the house, and seek diligently till she find it? And when she hath found it, she calleth her friends and her neighbours together, saying, Rejoice with me; for I have found the piece which I had lost. Likewise, I say unto you, there is joy in the presence of the angels of God over one sinner that repenteth.
>
> —LUKE 15:8–10

The parable now introduces a good woman who has lost one of her ten pieces of silver. In order to grasp the significance of her loss, we must understand what that silver coin represented. In Jesus' day, married women did not wear wedding rings as we do today to represent a covenant vow of faithfulness between a man and woman who marry. According to Bible custom, a virtuous married woman wore a necklace containing ten pieces of silver. That necklace was significant because it identified her as a virtuous woman.

If a woman was caught in adultery, she was brought to the gates of the city, and there the rulers of the city took off one piece of her silver. When people saw her on the street without the tenth piece of silver in her necklace, they recognized her as an adulteress. If through carelessness she lost a piece of her silver, her reputation as a virtuous woman was threatened. That is why the woman called for a light and a broom and swept until she found her lost coin. She wasn't about to go outside her home with nine pieces of silver around her neck and have everyone who saw her label her an adulteress.

Bible scholars generally agree that the "good woman" in the Scriptures represents the church in type. The woman in this parable was a good woman who through carelessness had lost her identity. The church at one time wore her label of holiness and chastity and lived a life that was different from the way the rest of the world lived. In the days of Charles Finney, people tipped their hats as he walked down the street because of the solemnity of the anointing that was upon this man of God. When he walked into a factory, people fell to the ground because of the power of the Holy Spirit that was on his life. Taverns shut down, movies went out of business, and godliness prevailed over worldliness in whole cities. A study of revivals throughout history reveals similar results in many lives and even entire cities being transformed to godly lifestyles.

Today the church is being shamed in the media and before the world because of the reproach that has been brought by religious leaders who have lost their identification of holiness and righteousness. Many in the church have decided they want to look, smell and walk like people in the world who don't know God. Through carelessness, apathy and compromise with the world, the church has lost her piece of silver and is bearing the reproach of being adulterous. We need to do as the woman in the parable and call for a light and a broom and begin to sweep until we regain possession of our lost silver, our identification as a holy people.

Scripture refers to silver as a type of redemption. Malachi writes, "And he shall sit as a refiner and purifier of silver: and he shall purify the sons of Levi, and purge them as gold and silver, that they may offer unto the LORD an offering in righteousness" (Mal. 3:3). God is putting His church into a crucible of circumstances and applying heat to allow the dross to come to the top and be purged. Jesus is coming for a holy church, not a worldly one. The message of holiness is sounding loud and clear in the church, for God is calling His people to repent of carelessness and compromise with the world to walk in faithfulness with Jesus, their true Bridegroom.

The woman in the parable diligently swept the house until she found her silver that was lost. We see the church being swept as God is tearing down men's kingdoms and exposing sin. It is incredible what the light of the Holy Spirit exposes. Revival starts with housecleaning, shaking and cleansing. We must quit being religious so we can truthfully say, "It is not the preacher or the deacon, but it's me, O Lord, standing in the need of prayer. I need a broom and a light. Inside me there are things that I have been covering up, places where I have compromised, so that I have lost my identification as a faithful follower of Christ. The world doesn't recognize me as different from them."

Identification is one of the greatest doctrines of the Bible; it matters that you are who you say you are. It doesn't matter what people think of you or how religious you are. *What matters is who you are in the presence of God.* The beginning of revival is calling for a light, then sweeping, cleaning and repenting. May you be willing to ask God to send the light into your spirit for Him to show you what is there. Then when that white light of God's judgment comes inside of you, you are going to know where to sweep with the broom. You must spend time being honest before God. If there is dirt in your temple, something you don't want the Lord to see, then call for the broom. Many people have a lot of dirt they are excusing by blaming their husband or wife or saying they have been this way all their lives. "My mother was this way; my daddy was this way." We don't belong to that daddy any longer. We belong to the family of God. We know we need to be cleansed and washed to have revival and be restored to our true identification.

The lost son

Jesus concluded this parable by telling of the lost son:

> A certain man had two sons: And the younger of them said to his father, Father, give me the portion of goods that falleth to me. And he divided unto them his living. And not many days after the younger son gathered all together, and took his journey into a far country, and there wasted his substance with riotous living.
>
> —Luke 15:11–13

This boy was a *son* living in the father's house. We have heard it taught that he was a sinner who came home to God. This message can be applied in that way, giving us a revelation of the loving Father's heart, which is ready to forgive. However, as we consider the fact that this boy was a son, leaving home with the gifts he received from the father, we can see more clearly what has happened in the church.

As a son he did something foolish. He asked his father to give him the inheritance he was entitled to receive, which the father did. It was the younger son who decided to leave, the one who was less mature. In his immaturity, he perhaps thought he had all he needed in the gifts the father gave him and that he could live better without the father's interference. The father's heart must have ached, but because of his desire to have a son who was mature, he let him go.

There was an attitude in many who were involved in the Charismatic movement of God that closely parallels the attitude of this younger son. The gifts of God were supremely important, as well as ministries and inheritances. People felt it was within their rights as sons of God to demand material prosperity as well as spiritual gifts and to develop their own ministries. The Book says that the younger son went out and spent his inheritance on riotous living. That is, he was hilariously living it up. Many pastors, including me, have had people come to us and say that they felt led to go out and exercise *their own ministries*. They took their portion, their inheritance or gifts, and put up signs all over the city: "Man of Power: Come and See My Miracles." The more spectacular their miracles were, the more people followed them.

I am not discounting the work of the Holy Spirit in the Charismatic movement, for thousands of lives were brought into a new experience of reality during that time. However, the attitude I am describing prevailed among many who were involved in Charismatic ministries. It is true that we all have a right to the inheritance, and we have received gifts. The Holy Spirit brought twenty-one gifts to the church when He came, and they belong to us. But too often we have become enthralled with the *gifts* and have lost sight of the *Giver*. How much better it would have been for the younger son to have stayed at home with the father. Instead, he squandered his wealth, and when famine came, he had nothing to eat. The Charismatic movement has come to an end, and many find themselves empty and hungry, with nothing to eat.

Many in the church have gone down to the swine pen to feed on husks. When someone preaches on the radio that if you will send him twenty dollars he will send you a string to tie around your waist so you can lose weight, that is a pigpen. When they offer to sell water from the Jordan where John baptized as holy water, or offer to send oil from a tree that was used to anoint Elijah, that is a disgrace. That is not preaching the living Word, which is bread for the hungry soul. The Book tells us the son "came to his senses." Some will have to go by way of the pigpen to come to their senses. Some who do go that way will be too proud to repent. However, there are those who are humbling themselves, repenting and being restored.

Now the church is getting hungry for the Word, for fresh bread that comes from the Father's house. "When he came to his senses," this son realized that the servants in his father's house had bread to eat while he was starving in a pigpen. Coming to his senses brought him to an attitude of repentance. This is the hour that repentance must come to the church. More than just saying, "I am sorry," repentance is letting God break our hearts over our sins until we are willing to confess, "Father, I have sinned against God and the church; I have been more interested in myself and my ministry than anything else. I am hungry, and no one can satisfy me except You, because there is a place created in me for God that no one else can fill."

Hallelujah! The church is coming home to the Father. This time we will not be satisfied with knowing the redemptive work of our Lord or the gifts of the Holy Spirit. I believe the next revelation coming to the church will be a revelation of our Father. Jesus came to unveil the Father to us.

When the boy came to his senses, he was willing to return to his father's house as a *servant*, saying he was no longer worthy to be called a son. His tone was totally different now; the strut had been taken out of him. He was not flipping his Bible, saying, "Look at me; I'm the person God raised up, and no one else in the world can do what I can do."

He had been stripped and was returning with his head down, crying, "I'm hungry, and I am going back to my daddy's house." He wanted to sit down with his father and eat with him. When you are willing to be made a servant, the Father's house will open to you. The father had to let this boy go to the swine pen and exhaust all his gifts, his power and anointing before he finally came to himself. When he had exhausted his resources and was starving to death in the swine pen, he thought of his father's house and could almost smell the fresh bread being prepared there. He arose to make the journey home, defeated, broken and humiliated, ready to become a servant in his father's house. However, he could not have anticipated the reception that awaited him there.

> But when he was yet a great way off, his father
> saw him, and had compassion.
> —LUKE 15:20

The father had been watching for his son, aching in his own heart because of the suffering he knew his son must be experiencing. Not only was the father watching for him, but he had gifts to give to him as well. These gifts were far better than those the son required when he left home, because they would last forever. When he saw his son trudging his weary way home, the father ran to him and *kissed him.* The gift of that kiss of reconciliation meant that everything was all right between them.

The kiss is one of the most beautiful ways to express deep, intimate love. There is nothing on earth as wonderful as knowing that there has been reconciliation between you and your Father. One of my greatest experiences in God was the first time I was able to say to my heavenly Father, "Please put Your arms around me and let me feel Your kiss." After being born again, loving God with all my heart and preaching the old-fashioned Methodist faith for nineteen years, I trembled the first time I ever asked Him to let me feel His kiss for fear it was blasphemous. But something inside me cried out for my heavenly "Daddy" to put His arms around me.

We had been having a move of God for about a week in our Bible school, with the students and faculty praying around the clock. I had been waiting in the presence of God, and I cried out to Him, "Please put Your arms around me." I felt His kiss; then I understood the cry of the bride in the Song of Solomon, "Let him kiss me with the kisses of his mouth" (Song of Sol. 1:2). When He kissed me, He left me with His Word. The day is coming when the church is going to receive the kiss of reconciliation from the Father and know deeper revelation of His Word.

Then the father requested that the *best robe* be brought to his repentant son. This robe was special, one the father had been saving. In many countries, when a king gets ready to take a bride, he has a special dress made for her with a beautiful design embroidered around the bottom and around the sleeves and neck that matches the design of his own robe. It has the crest, the governmental seal and everything that is on his robe, but is made in a smaller design to fit her. When she stands beside him to be presented as the queen, she has on a robe designed exactly like the king's robe.

Our heavenly Father has been working on it, too. "She shall be brought unto the king in raiment of needlework" (Ps. 45:14). The church has been embroidering it with the threads of the trials of her life, and every thread she has woven in her testing has embroidered His image into her robe. One day when the Bridegroom presents His bride, she will be found wearing His robe.

Then the father said, "Bring the *ring*." In Scripture,

the ring signifies authority as a power of attorney. Joseph was given the ring of Pharaoh, and with it the power of second in command. In the Book of Esther, the king's ring was taken from wicked Haman and given to Mordecai, who is a type of the Holy Spirit, ruling in righteousness. The ring was dipped into hot wax and pressed onto a written decree. According to the law, any decree sealed with the stamp of the king's ring could not be reversed.

Our Father is going to put a ring on the church's finger. He is calling us to prayer, getting ready for the Holy Spirit to stamp with hot wax His answer to the "fervent prayer of a righteous man [that] availeth much" (James 5:16). That is "hot wax" prayer. He is going to let the church take the ring that He puts on her finger and use it to answer her prayers. That ring will give us authority over the devil. I believe the church is going to have power such as we have never known to work miracles. People are going to be healed and delivered as the church uses her ring of authority to declare that she is taking territory from the devil.

Sandals were a significant gift of the father to his son, for they represented his status of sonship. In Bible times, when someone was disowned and lost his sonship, he took off his shoes. Servants who were not sons did not wear shoes. The church is called to walk in the light, in love, in the truth, in holiness and in the Spirit. The key word in the Book of Ephesians is the "walk" of the church, which reveals our sonship.

These gifts were all a vital part of the precious reception the loving father gave to his prodigal son. However, receiving the kiss, wearing the robe of righteousness, putting the ring on his finger and having shoes on his feet could not satisfy his *hunger*. The father called for a feast to be made, and they rejoiced together around a banquet table over the return of this lost son. The church is getting ready to have a revival that will feed hungry sons who are returning to the Father's house. They will receive gifts because of their brokenness and willingness to live as servants in the Father's house. With a servant spirit they can enjoy the robe of righteousness and be trusted with the ring of authority. Living in reconciliation with the Father, they will walk in the stature of true sonship.

This younger son had learned, through failure, to value the father's presence and enjoy a relationship with him. Unfortunately, the elder son in the parable had not developed that relationship, though he had stayed in the father's house. He became angry and critical of his father's relationship to this younger son who had obviously "blown it." The attitude of the elder brother serves as a warning to many in the church who are in danger of missing the next move of God. They refuse to go into the banquet to rejoice with the father, even though he comes to request their presence. It seems that every generation in church history that has experienced a great move of God has failed to go into the next move that God brings. In every move of God, some have said, "We don't want to go on. This is not the way we did it fifty years ago."

The director of one of our national Bible colleges attended my meetings in New Jersey some years ago. After I preached, he stood up and said to me, "I don't know your age, but I would call you a senior saint." He said that he had never seen a senior saint out on the cutting edge of what God is currently doing as he had seen me that day and that most of the older people he knew lived in what "used to be." He continued, "Here is a woman on the edge of prophetic truth who is telling us what is going to happen." He raved on until I was embarrassed, while he stood and declared to everyone present, "I shall not be left behind. I'm going to be on the cutting edge of what God is doing and learn to hear what the Spirit is saying to the church at this hour." Age doesn't have anything to do with going on with God. What matters is that we are able to see and hear what God is saying and doing. Then we must respond with the joy of the Father's heart in restoring sons to His house, instead of allowing the attitude of the elder brother to rule us.

A TIME OF GREAT REJOICING

There was great rejoicing over finding the lost sheep, the lost coin and the lost son. Each time there is a "found" person, there is great rejoicing. The Word teaches us concerning celebration, worship and dancing before the Lord. In the Father's house, there is a banquet with music and merriment to celebrate the joy of His heart at the return of His son. I didn't receive the understanding of celebration in a classroom situation. As I wrote earlier, God healed me from a deathbed. I was in braces, and God put my backbone together in seven places. He healed me in a Pentecostal meeting when I was a Methodist preacher, and when God struck me with Holy Ghost power, I danced before the Lord, although I didn't believe in it.

There is a controversy in the church today about praise and worship. A young pastor made an appointment to see me regarding a difficulty he was having with his leaders. He related to me that he had been reproved by his denominational conference because they did not approve of the praise and worship his church was experiencing. This young pastor showed these men what the Scriptures teach regarding dancing before the Lord, and they replied, "We can't help what the Book says; our conference doesn't believe in it."

My response to this young minister was, "If the Book says it, I will die by it." We must give up our opinions and notions to accept what the Book says, or we will not be a part of the next move of God.

Celebration is part of the revival that is coming when holiness is restored and sons come home to the Father's house. We must be careful not to demonstrate the attitude of the elder brother and miss what the Father is doing in this hour. Celebration is God's desire for His redeemed church. The kingdom of God is "righteousness, and peace, and joy in the Holy Ghost" (Rom. 14:17). The shepherd celebrated the return of the lost sheep, and the woman called her friends to celebrate the finding of her silver. The father said it was right to celebrate because his son was alive again. The more we receive of the family spirit of God, the more we will celebrate our redemption.

The church is the purpose of God unfolded to fulfill His dream for a family that bears His image. The sacrifice of Calvary had guaranteed that God's purpose will be fulfilled, for "he shall see of the travail of his soul and shall be satisfied" (Isa. 53:11). Whatever crucible God has to use to cleanse His church will result, not in destruction, but in redemption to make her a glorious church without spot or wrinkle. There will be a people who will possess their inheritance and become a part of the culmination of God's dream.

Chapter 8

GOD'S PURPOSE FULFILLED

The revelation of God's eternal purpose opened to another dimension for me when God revealed a truth that literally changed my life. At that time He unfolded the mandate I felt to train leaders during the time of transition in the church. This happened a few months after I left Fountain Gate Ministries, the church I founded and pastored for seventeen years, to travel extensively in this training ministry. The Bible College of Fountain Gate Ministries was planning their graduation ceremonies the spring following my leaving and invited me to return as pastor emeritus to speak to the graduating class. I was delighted to accept the invitation. I had poured my life into these students and had felt this particular class had more potential to succeed in God than any we had previously graduated. I sought God earnestly to give me a life-changing message for these students to take with them into their fields of ministry.

Arriving a few days early, my husband and I enjoyed participating in many of the activities before the graduation ceremony on Sunday night. We stayed in the home of one of the elders of the church, a precious friend. After we spent an evening enjoying a meal together, I asked permission to stay in our hosts' spacious dining room to spend some time seeking God for what He wanted to say to that graduating class. Of course they granted that permission, and I spent the late hours of the night waiting on God.

My conversation with my Father began something like this: "Father, I want You to tell me what You want me to say to this graduating class. I didn't come here at the expense of this church just to fill up time and space." (I have never met anyone who ever remembered his graduation exercise address.) I didn't want merely to challenge that class—I wanted them to leave that school knowing God had spoken to them and that the message had changed their lives.

As I waited, my Father asked me to talk to Him about the wilderness through which Moses led the children of Israel. He wanted me to describe the people I saw in the wilderness. So I tried to recall everything I had ever learned about the people in the wilderness and proceeded to describe them. They were people who marched out of Egypt under the leadership and sovereignty of the almighty, omnipotent, omniscient, omnipresent God. Before going very far, however, they desired to go back to Egypt. They were murmurers, complainers and faultfinders who rebelled against the eleven sovereign ways that God visited His people to meet their needs. They made the golden calf, refused to believe the voice of the prophets and died in that wilderness.

WILDERNESS PEOPLE

After I finished my dismal description of those wilderness people, my Father said He wanted to talk to me about the wilderness in which I was living. He spoke to me concerning the economic status of our country, the political structure and corruption in our government and the religious world that is full of apathy and love for materialism. He spoke of the moral status of this wilderness with its promiscuous sex, the curse of AIDS and the sin of abortion. He gave me a panoramic view of things that are happening in the wilderness of our nation. Then He said, "On two occasions in history I have invaded this world with a deliverer. The first time I invaded the world in answer to My peoples' cry and sent Moses to deliver them from Egypt. When Moses was born, the Egyptians were killing the male babies. The second time I invaded this world, I sent My Son to deliver My people out of darkness. At the time of Jesus' birth, there was also a decree to kill the male babies. Both times Satan thought he had killed My deliverers. My daughter, I am about to invade the world again, and they are killing babies again. But they are not going to destroy My deliverer, for He is the Head of the church, and My plan cannot be thwarted."

THE JOSHUA GENERATION

When my Father had thoroughly established in my thinking the wilderness in which I was living, He focused my attention again on that historical wilderness, asking me if all I saw in that wilderness were the murmurers, complainers and faultfinders. Then He began to describe another generation that was in that wilderness, one that had been born to the murmurers and complainers, trained by the wilderness testing to depend on God. They knew what it meant to have fresh bread every morning from the Father's hand, and they drank water from the rock. They didn't bow to idols, and they were clothed and fed by God, depending on Him for all their needs. My Father instructed me to think about the "Joshua generation" that had conquered the giants of the Promised Land. "That Joshua genera-tion is alive in your wilderness today," He said, "and they will receive their inheritance and have a part in fulfilling My eternal purpose."

I listened intently to what He was saying. It was as though I had never seen that new generation before. The Father declared to me that He was getting ready to take this Joshua generation into the land. We are living in the most exciting time this world has ever known. Our gen-eration has seen the faithfulness and power of the omnipotent, triune God in the middle of this present wilderness, sustaining such a vast number by supplying them daily bread and giving them to drink from the Rock. I can tell young people that they are living in the greatest hour that has ever been known in the church history. They are going to help take this new gen-eration in to possess the inheritance.

Earnestly wanting to understand what He was showing me, I asked my Father, "What *is* the inher-itance?" I told Him that I had heard some people refer to the land of Canaan as a "building program" for their church. They call the new facilities their "Canaan." Others refer to the inheritance of the promised land as the victorious, Spirit-filled life. It is true that as indi-viduals we must live holy lives, conquering the "ites" or our self lives, possessing the land through our obedi-ence. However, that is not the full meaning of receiving our inheritance. Many of our songs and hymns depict Canaan as heaven, the final destination for weary pilgrims. But Canaan cannot represent heaven, for there are neither giants to conquer in heaven nor battles to win in the presence of the throne of God. I felt I needed a clearer understanding of the reality of the inheritance God had promised to give the Joshua generation of today.

In answer to my question, my Father asked me to go back with Him into the eons of eternity, before time began, and witness the covenant made in the Godhead that was designed to bring to pass Their desire for a family. That covenant is the mystery revealed to Paul and is to be fulfilled by the church, the body of Christ. Paul declared:

> Christ also loved the church, and gave himself for it; that he might sanctify and cleanse it with the washing of water by the word, that he might present it to himself a glorious church, not having spot, or wrinkle, or any such thing; but that it should be holy and without blemish.
>
> —Ephesians 5:25–27

Paul taught that "Christ is the head of the church" (Eph. 5:23). He also taught that God gave the fivefold ministry to the church for the perfecting of the saints, for the edifying of the body of Christ, "till we all come in the unity of the faith, and of the knowledge of the Son of God, unto a perfect man, unto the measure of the stature of the fulness of Christ" (Eph. 4:13). As unfathomable as it may seem, the Father is going to have a family in the church who will bear His image.

The inheritance that was partially received in

Joshua's generation serves as a type of the promise that is going to be fulfilled in reality in this new generation. The time came when God took Moses home and told Joshua He wanted him to take the generation into Canaan that He had been training in the wilderness. The Scripture presents Joshua as a humble man who had no personal goals other than to please God. He dealt with sin immediately and with finality, and for every successful battle he gave God the glory. He was resourceful in courage, strong in faith and wholeheartedly committed to God and His law. As a leader he showed the way without fear, conquering the land and dividing the inheritance. God is still calling men and women today whose hearts are like Joshua's.

There were some arduous tasks assigned to Joshua, some that many of us would not have wanted. It was time for the children of Israel to begin to receive their inheritance if they were willing. They were being confronted with the decision: Were they willing to go into the Promised Land? According to the Book, we find that the first generation as a whole decided they didn't want to go into the land God had promised them. As a result, they wandered for thirty-nine years and died in the wilderness. They were those who had come out of Egypt but were overcome by the "system" of the wilderness. They do not represent sinners, for they had come out of Egypt to follow God. But they refused to go into the Promised Land, and they died in that wilderness.

There are some in the church today who are being overcome by the system of the world, worshiping golden calves, rebelling and taking part in gossip, criticism, church splits, murmuring and faultfinding. They do not really know their God. They know *about* Him, but they have no intimate relationship with Him. Though they will not return to Egypt, they will surely perish in the wilderness. There are others like Michal, King David's wife, who mocked David when he worshiped hilariously. She was struck with barrenness, the worst curse that could come to a Jewish woman. There are those like the elder son in the backyard of the prodigal's home, who was a murmurer and complainer and did not join the celebration. He was at the father's house, but he did not rejoice with the father at the return of the prodigal son.

No one can keep you from having what God has ordained you to have except yourself. You are responsible to choose to receive your inheritance. I have never met a man or woman, church or family, nor have I seen a job or profession that is worth my missing God's inheritance. When I understood God's purpose, I determined that no one was worth what it would cost me to miss it. When that kind of determination motivates you, you will enter into your inheritance.

The first generation had died without receiving their inheritance, and now God was preparing to take their sons and daughters into the Promised Land.

> And Joshua said, Hereby ye shall know that the living God is among you, and that he will without fail drive out from before you the Canaanites, and the Hittites, and the Hivites, and the Perizzites, and the Girgashites, and the Amorites, and the Jebusites.
>
> —JOSHUA 3:10

CONFRONTING THE ENEMIES

The Father's plan was to give them their inheritance by driving out the enemies that dwelt in the land. God also said, "Every place that the sole of your foot shall tread upon, that have I given unto you" (Josh. 1:3). The command God gave was twofold. God was going to run out some of the "ites," but Israel had to *possess* the land in order to receive their inheritance. Joshua's generation did not enter into their full inheritance because they didn't conquer all the "ites." Canaan was a type of the real inheritance God ordained for the church, as the Old Testament is a shadow of that which is to be fulfilled in reality in the New Testament.

When the Holy Spirit told Paul to leave Jerusalem and go to the desert of Arabia, this newly converted apostle was preaching the gospel as he understood it. He had been transformed by the power of God, apprehended to preach to the Gentiles, and he was preaching his Pentecostal message. (Some of our churches are still doing that.) God had apprehended Paul for more than that, however, for He had been waiting since before the foundation of the world to reveal His mystery to the heart of man.

In that desert, Paul had an encounter with the infinite, almighty, omnipotent God who rolled out His eternal purpose and revealed it to the apostle "born out of due season." The Old Testament Book of Joshua has its fulfillment in Paul's letter to the Ephesians in the New Testament. The heart of God was unveiled to Paul concerning the mystery that had been hidden in God since before the foundation of the world. God had cherished in His heart from eternity His desire for a family, and He revealed to Paul that desire and His plan to fulfill it through the church. That which God ordained is contained in the biblical words *predestination, foreordination, predetermination, precounsel* and *elect*, as well as other similar words. Paul said he was apprehended that he might preach that mystery that was with God from the beginning and not able to be revealed until now.

The church is going to receive its inheritance, "according to the eternal purpose which he purposed in Christ Jesus" (Eph. 3:11). Paul declared:

> I became a servant of this gospel by the gift of God's grace given me through the working of his power…to preach to the Gentiles the unsearchable riches of Christ, and to make plain to everyone the administration of this mystery, which for ages past was kept hidden in God…His intent was that now, *through the church,* the manifold wisdom of God should be made known to the rulers and authorities in the heavenly realms, according to his eternal purpose which he accomplished in Christ Jesus our Lord.
> —EPHESIANS 3:7–11, NIV, EMPHASIS ADDED

These "rulers and authorities in the heavenly realms" are not the wicked host we see in Ephesians chapter 6. These principalities are the heavenly hosts—all the saints who have gone on. Paul said that through the church the manifold wisdom of God was going to be made known to them. Throughout his epistles Paul writes about this mystery of the church that is going to be triumphant and take back what belongs to her. Jesus came to heal the brokenhearted, to set the captives free and to open the eyes of the blind. We have seen glimpses of that reality, but not as we will see it. The church is going to have a revival that will not have men's names tagged on it, for Jesus Himself is going to be revealed in the church.

At present, the church is in a transitional period. The Charismatic era is coming to a close, not to be destroyed, but to be built upon. We are on the threshold of stepping into the last great era when we are going to have a mighty visitation of God, and the church will receive its inheritance. We will see the church:

> ...grow up into him in all things, which is the head, even Christ: from whom the whole body fitly joined together and compacted by that which every joint supplieth, according to the effectual working in the measure of every part, maketh increase of the body unto the edifying of itself in love.
>
> —EPHESIANS 4:15–16

This move of God will include those of today's Joshua generation who are walking where He is walking, hearing what He is hearing and moving where He is moving—not those who are merely attending church. Men and women of God all over the world are aware that the church is in transition between the old move of God and the new move that is coming, when the church will come into its inheritance, and the Father will have a family that is conformed to the image of His Son.

Scripture is very clear regarding our responsibility as part of the Joshua generation who want to enter into our inheritance.

> Every place that the sole of your foot shall tread
> upon, that have I given unto you...There shall
> not any man be able to stand before thee all the
> days of thy life: as I was with Moses, so I will be
> with thee: I will not fail thee, nor forsake thee...
> This book of the law shall not depart out of thy
> mouth; but thou shalt meditate therein day and
> night, that thou mayest observe to do according
> to all that is written therein: for then thou shalt
> make thy way prosperous, and then thou shalt
> have good success.
>
> —JOSHUA 1:3, 5, 8

Before the people of the new generation were ready
to receive their inheritance, they had to be tested by life
in the wilderness. God is training the church through
testing today. Some have taught that the saints aren't
supposed to have trials and testing, but testing is necessary to reveal our lack of character and bring us to the
place where we can receive His character. God doesn't
test us to find out who we are, for He already knows
that. We don't know who we are until God takes us
through the testing and we see our response. The
wilderness we are in is God's classroom. When it looks
black and hopeless we may be tempted to think that
God doesn't love us. To the contrary, He loves us so
much He is training us to bring us to spiritual maturity
so that we can receive our inheritance.

STEPPING INTO MATURITY

The first step to spiritual maturity is *crisis*. Crisis cre-
ates in us a *hunger*, which is the second step to maturity. Then follows a *searching* during which we receive

revelation. Revelation brings us to *realization,* and we are able to enter into *service* and *obedience* in a mature walk in Christ. We will never find out how big our God is until we have to prove Him in a crisis. He is not going to ask us to possess the land and war against the giants without first training us in the wilderness. He gives us grace every step of the way, carrying us as lambs in His bosom. Only those who have been fully sustained in their hearts through testing and trials can submit to Joshua's leadership. We must qualify, or be proven, to receive our inheritance.

As we have seen, "Canaan" does not refer to heaven, for there are no giants or "enemies" in heaven. The enemies inside us are the "ites" that hinder us from being changed into the image of God and thereby receiving our inheritance as a part of His family. We must conquer them in order to experience the love of God in the family of God. Contention, jealousy, outbursts of wrath, selfishness, ambitions, desires to rule, dissensions, heresies, envy, murder, drunkenness and the like are all "ites" that keep us from our inheritance. (See Galatians 5:19–21.) To run out the "ites" means to run out all forms of adultery as well, such as carrying on an affair with your own flesh as well as with someone who does not belong to you. All fornication, uncleanness, hatred and unforgiveness must be purged from these temples of the Holy Ghost that Christ may receive glory in the church, His body.

The Spirit of God is speaking regarding unforgiveness as I have never heard Him speak in all my years of ministry. We must be forgiven of God, and we must forgive everyone who has offended us. At one time my

Father asked me to write to a certain minister to ask for his forgiveness. I can truthfully say I never did anything that I know of to hurt that minister. I esteemed him, even though through "prophecy" he had led a large number of my parishioners to leave the church I was pastoring. I felt that he was the one who had offended through that situation, and all I did in response was to stand aloof from him. But God dealt with the attitude in me and told me to ask the man's forgiveness for demanding innocence of him instead of being willing to accept his need to receive forgiveness.

I did what my Father asked, and through that obedience my temple was cleansed of one more "ite." A few weeks later, I was in awe at the new revelation that was flooding my own soul. As I was thanking God for it, He showed me that because of my obedience in writing that letter of forgiveness, a flow of power and truth had been released from the heavenlies to my own heart. God promises to equip us, and one by one we are going to overcome these enemies of our souls.

God's church will march triumphantly into her inheritance. Do you think Jesus is not going to have what the Father planned? The church is going to follow the example of Joshua and destroy the Hittites, Girgashites, Canaanites, Hivites, Amalekites, "back-bites" and all other "ites" that are enemies that keep us from possessing our inheritance. My Father told me to go as a mother in Israel to help leaders to sharpen their swords and to prepare to take His people into the land of promise where God's dream will be fulfilled.

I thought that was the end of the message, but it wasn't. Some time later, my Teacher whispered to me that He wanted me to go back and read that passage in Joshua again because I had not seen everything He wanted me to see. He told me to look in the Book to see *when* Joshua was going into the land. I read:

> Pass through the host, and command the people, saying, Prepare you victuals; for within three days ye shall pass over this Jordan, to go in to possess the land, which the LORD your God giveth you to possess it.
>
> —JOSHUA 1:11

God commanded Joshua to prepare the people, for in *three days* they were going to enter the land.

In Scripture, the word *day* can refer to twenty-four hours or to an era of time. Peter wrote, "But beloved, be not ignorant of this one thing, that one day is with the Lord as a thousand years, and a thousand years as one day" (2 Pet. 3:8). If we apply that principle to our calendar, we would say that in the year 2000 our second "day" came to a close, and we entered the "third day" of our age. Our calendar is based on the history of the church, the year A.D. 1 beginning after Christ's resurrection.

It is quite exciting to follow the mention of the "third day" throughout the Bible. For example, Esther went before the king on the third day of prayer and fasting to plead with him to save her and her people. Mordecai was able to pronounce the hanging of Haman on the third day. Jesus turned the water into wine on the third day at the wedding in Cana. And before He died, He said, "Destroy this temple, and in three days I will raise it up" (John 2:19). The Jews thought He meant His own body. But He didn't build His own body—He is building the church. He is the Head of the church, which is

His body. The prophet spoke in the Book of Hosea
regarding the third day:

> Come, and let us return unto the LORD: for he
> hath torn, and he will heal us; he hath smitten,
> and he will bind us up. After two days will he
> revive us: in the third day he will raise us up, and
> we shall live in his sight. Then shall we know, if
> we follow on to know the LORD: his going forth
> is prepared as the morning; and he shall come
> unto us as the rain, as the latter and former rain
> unto the earth.
>
> —HOSEA 6:1–3

People who are hearing the voice of God know that
He is going to do something soon. I said, "Now Lord,
don't let me go out into left field by projecting a
timetable for Your moving." I don't know how long the
third day is going to last, but the church is getting ready
to enter the third day. Every time we write the date, we
are saying that we have entered into the third day on our
calendar. And we know the church is going into her
inheritance, for Scripture teaches that Jesus is coming
for a glorious church without spot or wrinkle.

In the literal history of the Book of Joshua, the
people never received all of their inheritance. They
went into the Promised Land, but they married the
"ites" instead of conquering them, and they never pos-
sessed the mountainous areas. "This time," God said to
me, "the church is not going to marry the 'ites.' She is
going to possess the land." This is the greatest hour the
church has ever known. Our command now is to get
our "vittles" ready, get our sword sharpened, come to
maturity in Christ and let the church be the church.

The Father is going to bring the church into that which the triune Godhead ordained before the foundation of the world. That intertheistic covenant that the Godhead swore together will not be broken, and no demon, devil or denomination will be able to keep the Son from receiving His inheritance. We must become that church without spot or blemish, one mature man, grown up into our Head, which is Christ. Relating to the typology of Joshua, we must possess the land, conquering all the enemies of our souls, following our heavenly Joshua's battle plans, until we enter into all of our inheritance.

God had given me a life-changing message. It birthed a cry in the hearts of that graduation class to become a part of the new generation, and many of them are serving on foreign mission fields today. This message is consuming me as I travel across the nation to fulfill the mandate of God to help prepare His leaders and His people to come into their inheritance. It is a message that can be life changing for everyone who believes the eternal purpose of God. All who dare to respond to the working of the Holy Spirit will find themselves becoming a wonderful part of fulfilling God's purpose.

Enjoy your journey
with God!

Dr. Fuchsia Pickett has been referred to as one of the "best Bible teachers of our time," and now you know why!

We pray that you have been inspired with the life message found in *God's Purpose for You*, and we know you'll enjoy two more opportunities to sit under her anointed teaching and draw closer to God.

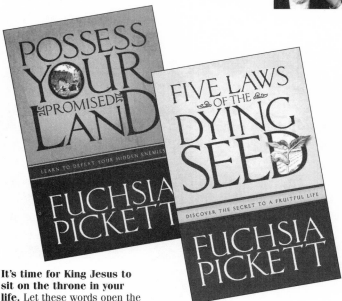

It's time for King Jesus to sit on the throne in your life. Let these words open the gates of your soul through obedience and unlock the gates of your spirit with faith.

Step into righteousness. Uncover God's grace, deliverance, timing and patience. Walk through the seasons of life, and cast aside worldly hindrances.